T0063560

RETAIL REBRANDED

27 secrets of market leaders

Angie Bell

BALBOA.
PRESS
A DIVISION OF HAY HOUSE

Copyright © 2014 Bell Retail Solutions.

All rights reserved. No part of this book may be used or reproduced by any means, graphic, electronic, or mechanical, including photocopying, recording, taping or by any information storage retrieval system without the written permission of the publisher except in the case of brief quotations embodied in critical articles and reviews.

Graphics/Art Credit: Trudi Grogan.
boxadvertising.com.au

Balboa Press books may be ordered through booksellers or by contacting:

Balboa Press
A Division of Hay House
1663 Liberty Drive
Bloomington, IN 47403
www.balboapress.com.au
1 (877) 407-4847

Because of the dynamic nature of the Internet, any web addresses or links contained in this book may have changed since publication and may no longer be valid. The views expressed in this work are solely those of the author and do not necessarily reflect the views of the publisher, and the publisher hereby disclaims any responsibility for them.

The author of this book does not dispense medical advice or prescribe the use of any technique as a form of treatment for physical, emotional, or medical problems without the advice of a physician, either directly or indirectly. The intent of the author is only to offer information of a general nature to help you in your quest for emotional and spiritual well-being. In the event you use any of the information in this book for yourself, which is your constitutional right, the author and the publisher assume no responsibility for your actions.

Printed in the United States of America.

ISBN: 978-1-4525-1317-1 (sc)
ISBN: 978-1-4525-1316-4 (e)

Balboa Press rev. date: 02/22/2014

for Ros

Contents

Foreword   by Dr. Dale Miller

Retailing is a very exciting and very challenging area of contemporary business. Successful retailing has many benefits – not only for the owners but also for employees, customers, suppliers and the broader community. It is often one of the largest private sector employers in many developed countries. In emerging economies, micro retailers, selling their own products and services, are embarking on a path to economic self-sufficiency and community contribution.

The long history of retailing has caught the imagination of television producers with recent series on Selfridges, the iconic department store opened in London in 1909, and The Paradise, an Anglicised version of Émile Zola's fictional account of the Bon Marché [Au Bonheur des Dames (The Ladies' Paradise)]. Moreover, the public response to these shows has been very positive and suggests that customers and the community at large, are fascinated by retailing. People are interested in retailing stories and what we can call retail heritage or history. Good news for pro-active retailers aiming to provide not only products and services, but also a total retail experience for their customers.

Developing that experience often draws on the background of the business, where over time the retailer builds up a strong reputation and retailer (corporate) brand. Whether a long standing business or relatively new, retailers can draw on their backgrounds to reinforce their brand.

Retailers and researchers alike are very interested in ongoing developments to improve retail practices and performance. One area attracting a lot of contemporary research attention is the area of rebranding.

We are talking here of the firm. Although rebranding products is certainly of interest to retailers, it is generally a process for manufacturers and suppliers, with some consultation with retailers. You will be aware of many retailers who have reinvented, revitalised or refreshed their businesses. Rebranding is much more than a changed name or logo. To treat a makeover for your business in such a way would be to seriously underestimate what is needed to reinvigorate a retail brand.

This book takes a retailer-focused approach – a practical approach to reviving your business for the benefit of multiple stakeholders. Angie Bell draws on her own extensive experiences to offer practical options for reviving your brand. Whether your business is in storefront retailing, online retailing or both, you can consider the advice that is offered here.

I encourage you to read this book in the context of your own current business and your own previous experience.

Happy Rebranding!

Dr. Dale Miller
January 2014

> '*New forms of retailing continue to emerge either to lead or to meet customer demands. Existing retailers must review and reshape their strategic directions in the face of these innovations*.'[1]

Dr. Dale Miller. Global branding expert, Griffith University Gold Coast, Australia.

Introduction

What on earth is a quirky frog doing on the front cover and why is it pushing a shopping cart?

With over one third of all species now on the brink of extinction, the frog has a challenging and uncertain future. His environment is changing at a rapid rate never before seen and he must find ways to adapt and grow or fail and perish.

The very clever little frog that appears throughout this book *is* adapting. He stands out in the crowd as unique because he is able to reinvent himself to take on the challenges that lie ahead. He is a symbol for evolutionary change. He is a symbol for sustainable branding and he is my symbol for you, the specialty retailer.

Together, change and sustainability are steering the future just like your clever little frog is steering the shopping cart. Standing out in the crowd through uniqueness is what rebranding represents. The way forward for your brand is to be clear about who you are, what you do and how you do it. Developing a unique retail brand with attributes that help you continuously evolve in an ever-changing environment is the key to survival and indeed the key to growth.

Many retailers have experienced the downturn in business since the events of the 2008 global financial crisis. Your retail business model may have been very successful for some years until recently, when you are finding it difficult to make a living and competition is increasing. High rent to turnover ratios, increasing electricity and staffing costs, a sluggish economy, diminishing margins, lower foot traffic and lower sales volumes have resulted in many retailers failing.

Many specialty retailers are losing market share to market leaders and are now realising that doing the same thing no longer works. Perhaps your business is not moving forward and perhaps you are searching for some way to change your practices to help you stay in business and grow.

You may even be considering closing your doors and walking away from the business you have worked so hard to build. It's a heart-breaking scenario, but one that more than 3000 retailers throughout Australia alone faced in 2013. [2]

'A retail business model or RBM articulates how a retailer creates value for its customers and appropriates value from the markets'.[3] Today's most successful retailers have applied rebranding strategies to their RBM that have helped them pave the way forward to market share gains and sustainability. Rebranding your RBM through innovation and change will sustain and grow your business into the future.

You might feel like you don't have the resources to change. I will show you examples of retailers who have made changes on a shoestring budget. In fact, most of my clients have adjusted on very limited resources in a very short space of time with amazing results!

In the past twenty-five years I have had experience as a retailer, wholesaler, merchandiser, trainer, retail consultant and motivational speaker. In that time I have learnt that no matter what your size of business, if you incorporate best practice into every element of your RBM, you will achieve growth. I have learnt that specialty retailers *can* improve their business models, you *can* adapt and change and you *can* grow and evolve into the future.

Retail Rebranded will show you how to apply five key steps to reassess, reposition, rename, redesign and relaunch your retail brand towards growth. It will push you to think about adapting your business through sustainability and innovation in the competitive contemporary marketplace. It will challenge you to apply them to your own environment to gain your own unique brand positioning. It will help you construct and implement an action plan for change.

You may be reading this book because you wish to expand into new markets and update your image in order to grow. You may feel your retail brand has lost its competitive advantage due to the rapid changes in your surrounding retail landscape. Your retail brand may have become irrelevant, tired or outdated to your target markets and you suspect that it no longer serves you well. Perhaps it is simply not performing to your expectations and you can no longer make a profit.

Whatever your reason for considering change, **Retail Rebranded** can help you reshape your retail brand to compete more aggressively in a new standard of retail where you can be relevant, experiential, innovative, diverse and most of all, sustainable. It will help you stand out in the crowd just like your clever little frog!

In semester two of 2012 at Griffith University, I was enrolled in a course called *Retailer Innovation and Branding* delivered by Dr. Dale Miller. Dr. Miller helped me join all the dots from my work experience and see with absolute clarity the way forward for specialty retailers to adapt and grow. She opened my mind to wider thinking, greater possibilities and helped further develop my understanding of retail concepts and strategy.

On the last day of lectures, she went around the class and asked each of us to outline two key learnings from the course. Leaving me until very last she asked, 'How about you Angie, what did you learn?' I replied, 'Firstly, I believe that more specialty retailers need to think about applying innovation and sustainability to their business models, and I want to help more of them understand how they can do that. Secondly, the 20-25 year-old students surrounding me have much higher expectations from retailers than my generation and my parents' generation.

They have helped me see there is a great divide between what many of my clients [retailers] provide and what today's generation expects. I really want to help as many retailers as possible bridge the gap to revitalise their models so they can maintain relevance and grow into the future'.

Dr. Miller has studied and consulted to the iconic Australian retail brand 'David Jones' for many years and during that semester the retail giant was in the media for incorporating an omni-channel approach to its RBM. Omni-channel retailing aims to combine the advantages of online with traditional bricks and mortar and has been termed 'brick n click'. It meets consumer demands through a range of buying channels including in-store, online and mobile.

Dr. Miller's view is that department stores have always omni-channeled through mail order catalogues and home delivery services once enjoyed by consumers. She said we all stand to learn by looking back at what worked in the past and reinventing it for the future. Dr. Miller suggested that David Jones, Myer, Macy's, Selfridges and Harrods have all reinvented the mail order channel of the past as today's online channel.

That comment triggered my thinking about how I could get my rebranding message out to as many specialty retailers as possible to help you change, adapt and grow. As a result of my work with Dr. Miller, I have developed **Retail Rebranded**, an easy to read 5-step rebranding manual to help you reinvent, revitalise and revive your business model.

I will share 27 secrets of market leaders that show you how to adapt your retail brand to regain and maintain your relevance to your customers and progress you into the new era of retailing where competitive best practice is the name of the game.

Much of the time, I hear excuses from specialty retailers about why they can't change. *I can't price all my stock because the prices change too often and I don't have time. I can't replace my signage because the landlord won't let me. I can't train my staff because they won't stay back for two hours after closing. I can't move my counter because I will have to pay an electrician to move the wiring.* Although I have heard it all many times before, I still say *you can, you can, you can!*

I have witnessed specialty retailers update their stores completely in a single weekend at very little cost. They somehow manage to convince staff and friends to help them build slat walls, paint floors, price stock and move counters as part of their vision and plan to adapt and grow into diverse, flourishing, relevant and successful businesses with unbelievable sales growth.

You can choose to join those who say they can't change or be brave and invest in changes now that say you can. I hope you thoroughly enjoy the journey of reading the secrets that big retailers don't really want you to know, and apply some of these principles to your own retail empire to improve your business out of sight! *How exciting!*

1-reasses

There's never been a better time to **reassess** your RBM (retail business model). An analysis of the key areas of income (revenue streams), your supply chain, the changing consumer, sustainability and innovation gives you an opportunity to restructure, revise and reinvent which is a normal part of business strategy development.

Right now is a great time to start writing down some of your ideas and developing a to-do-list to help you get the ball rolling. Looking at all the possibilities helps you to see all your options more clearly. Sometimes, starting with a business SWOT analysis can be very helpful.

It's a simple exercise that requires you to be objective about your business in these four key areas. In the squares below, write down in general terms, what you think are your strengths, weaknesses, opportunities and threats. It's a good idea to use a pencil so you can amend your ideas as you work through the book and develop your new strategy as you read.

SWOT analysis

Strengths	Weaknesses
Opportunities	Threats

After completing this exercise, you should have a more strategic focus for planning and be thinking along the lines of moving forward through change. The Opportunities section is of great importance, as it may help you to see a way forward.

For example, you may be planning to open longer hours or to develop an e-commerce website that makes sales for you while you are relaxing at home with your family. You may be planning to move to a better location and pay less rent or to improve inefficiencies in order to run on less staff. You may be thinking about incorporating labor saving technological advancements in order to cut costs. This SWOT analysis simply highlights areas for you to mull over in your own context. The future is full of new and exciting challenges for specialty retailers, so *let's get to it and reshape your retail brand!*

To-do list

Secret 1-Take a mixed revenue approach

The past definition of retailing was bricks and mortar selling: your customers buying a specialty range of goods that you purchased at a trade price from a local or national supplier for resale and consumption.

Consider that the retail landscape or **retailscape** has changed forever. Gone are the boom pre-global financial crisis days. Sales of bricks and mortar retail may never return to those levels thanks to a number of factors. The Internet, economic, environmental, social and generational changes are now influencing consumer purchase behaviours. Contemplate that your retail business demands diversification and change to remain relevant as your omni-channel retail competitors, the consumer, technology and the information highway drive us all forwards.

One way to consider diversifying is through a **mixed revenue approach.** Think of your business as an apple pie with a number of slices that are all different serving sizes. Each slice makes up an ever-changing percentage of your revenue or income from a different segment. These slices evolve and morph over time but at the end of the year, add up to positive growth, *or weight gain!*

Diversifying revenue streams adds strength to your RBM just like it adds strength to a share or property portfolio. It mitigates the risk of relying on a sole income stream or sole supplier and allows you flexibility to change direction quickly if business conditions require.

As an example, let's say you are a florist located in a shopping centre. Your mixed revenue model or apple pie is divided into eight slices:

1. Store sales
2. Online sales
3. Phone orders and home deliveries
4. Interflora orders
5. Weddings
6. Funerals and special occasions
7. Hotel foyer arrangements
8. Supply to local fruit shops and mixed business for resale

The last two segments could be on your list to target for future growth. Of course, you can add or subtract whichever slice you like; *it's your apple pie!* These are simply ideas to get you thinking about additional market segments or revenue streams you can add to your already established business. Segmenting your revenue streams in this way allows focus and diversifies business structure to target development of each segment or slice. It enables clear goal setting and provides strategic direction for controlled growth. It also helps you identify strengthening or diminishing segments of your revenue.

Throughout the book, I share real stories and examples of today's retailers from around the world. Some of the stories are shining examples of inventive and proactive businesses that incorporate change and others are of experiences that have plenty of room for improvements!

Here is the first example outlining how a local specialty musical instrument store's revenue slices have changed since 2008. The store's owner has projected future growth and decline based on trending numbers. Note how the e-tail (electronic retail) channel, which was at zero in FY2008, grew to prop up the unprecedented trending decline of the traditional bricks and mortar retail channel and how the mobile commerce channel is predicted to grow rapidly. The challenge is to ask yourself how this concept can be applied to your business to facilitate sustainability and growth into the future.

'Music Express' percentage revenue analysis

Year	2008	2010	2015	2020
Retail	89	75	64	30
Education	10	10	10	15
Tuition	1	2	3	5
E-tail	0	13	22	30
Mobile-commerce	0	0	1	15
New category (acoustic pianos)		0	0	5

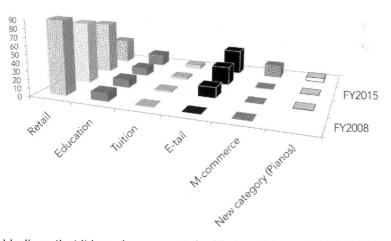

I believe that it is no longer sustainable to exist as a 100% bricks and mortar reseller with no supplementary revenue streams or additional sales channels. Market leaders have already diversified.

Now is the time for outside the square thinking to move forward incorporating diversification to enhance economic sustainability.

To get your thinking started, let's look at a few ways to diversify your revenue streams. Perhaps you can sublet a space in your premises to a complimentary business that increases foot traffic whilst decreasing overheads. 'Bigbox' retailers in America have been doing this since the 1990s with Starbucks and other complimentary retailers who not only pay rent for space within enormous stores, but add to the attractiveness and overall experience of the shopping destination.

In the Australian marketplace, Masters Home Improvements have incorporated McDonald's into some of their store locations. McDonald's not only pay rent for the space but the brand encourages customers to stay longer in-store and may even increase customer traffic *to* the store.

Department stores worldwide have been successfully using the store-within-a-store model for over a century where floor space is rented directly to manufacturer brands, particularly in fashion and cosmetics. Hairdressers often take this approach with nail technicians or beauty professionals who sublet a small floor space to minimise overhead costs.

Another Australian example is independent retailer 'Wallingtons' in Victoria who has incorporated this strategy by placing a national brand paint store within a 'bigbox' hardware, timber, gardening and pet store. This enhances both the diversity of the business model and the retail destination for customers. It allows the paint segment of the business to enjoy national marketing, better buying, merchandising programs, training and other benefits offered by the member group.

I recently read about a store in Melbourne's Fitzroy that sells French fashion during the day and converts the space to French conversation classes in the evening. This is a way to improve the rental return if you consider the increase that opening hours add to the turnover and profitability of the store whilst rental costs remain static or can be shared across two or more tenants. It makes sense to use the space for as many hours as possible, especially considering that your competitors on the Internet are open for business 24/7.

I know a pair of young brothers who recently signed a lease for a large floor space on main road frontage. They quickly split the premises in two, installed a coffee shop and lunchtime restaurant in one side and an evening pizza and mezze wine bar in the other, maximising opening hours and the return on rental costs.

Perhaps there is an opportunity to merge with a competitor to create a bigger and better experience for your customers and a stronger combined market position? Any way you can decrease the ratio of rent to turnover is a way towards economic sustainability.

Another way to think outside the square is to value-add your offer. We all know that the longer consumers spend in-store, the more chance they have of buying. It makes perfect sense for retailers to add value to the consumers' shopping experience where possible so that consumers are enticed to stay longer and buy more.

Swedish brand IKEA, for example, has 400-seat restaurants in stores worldwide to keep their customers in-store longer and retails the food it serves in the restaurant, in the grocery section. Now that's food demonstration retailing at its best where customers can taste before they buy!

The most successful furniture retailer in the world[4] has installed supervised children's playrooms where mum and dad can leave the kiddies while they shop the hours away. This positions IKEA as a direct competitor against nearby shopping centre destinations that offer food and entertainment for families on weekends and provides a unique shopping experience that enhances its brand positioning and its brand meaning to the consumer.

The retailer has thought about the needs of its target market and has provided solutions for them in order to increase average in-store shopping times to capitalise on selling opportunities. I read that the new upwardly mobile middle class consumer in China reportedly spends a whole day at IKEA to fully experience the brand before they buy. Mum can be found on a lounge chair reading a book, dad at a desk using his iPad and young son on the couch playing Nintendo. All day! *Yep. All day!* Now that's gotta be experiential retail branding at its best!

I have a client in outback Queensland, Australia who realised there was nowhere to get great coffee in town and so grabbed the opportunity to install a contemporary coffee and macaroon bar at the rear of their newly rebranded homewares store.[5] It has become a fashionable destination for locals and tourists alike. Coffee and homeware sales are booming and the store recently won an award for 2013 Retailer of the Year!

I have many specialist paint store clients who have installed up-to-date colour lounges with funky modern furniture and safe, interactive and fun playrooms for their customers' kids that keep parents engaged in colour selection for longer, translating to higher paint and wallpaper sales and creating a point of difference from their competitors.[6]

The question specialty retailers must ask is how can you provide a unique shopping experience that enhances the lives of your customers and gives you a competitive advantage?

Mountain view

A paint retailer located at the base of a mountain told me about how he had diversified his model to accommodate seasonal lines. To accommodate the downturn in winter, Leroy introduced Plasterboard to help him prosper through the difficult period. He targeted his trade paint customers. Leroy could have let his local hardware store supply the Plasterboard. Instead, he seized the opportunity to diversify his business model. It's not unlike the local ski hire shop transforming itself into a hiking gear shop in the summer months. Why not? **Diversifying your retail business model adds to your economic sustainability**

Secret 2-Diversify your supply chain

Supply chains are changing as market leading retailers cut out the middleman almost completely. Californian brand Apple supplies its own stores and has achieved worldwide price parity in doing so. Spanish clothing giant Zara is 20-30% cheaper than its competitors by sourcing directly from its factory in Spain. Swiss based brand Nespresso furnishes stores with coffee and machines that bear its own brand name. Canadian guitar makers Godin supply direct to retailers from their manufacturing plants, source their own raw materials and cut out distributors all together in all but two countries worldwide. IKEA own timber production plants that manufacture their furniture and incidentally, planted 2 million trees across America alone in 2012 to reduce their carbon footprint.[7] Walmart source a large portion of their stock through direct supply from manufacturers, as do Aldi, Woolworths, Masters, Bunnings and Coles. Billabong, Nike and countless other retailers all have a competitive advantage over traditional specialty retailers by incorporating the **vertical model of supply**.

A supply chain that is shortened enhances buy prices and lowers sell prices whilst increasing margins to the retailer. Granted it has problems to overcome for small business with sourcing, shipping, importing and warehousing. However, it's only a matter of time before this model and variations of it become the only way to compete in retail markets.

As technology improves, markets open and global freight costs are an expected part of doing business, distributors and suppliers will diminish in many sectors and manufacturers will increasingly supply direct to retailers and end-users [consumers] worldwide. This trend can be seen quite transparently in the food sector with supermarkets sourcing directly from farmers for their 'home' brands and websites such as foodorbit.com facilitating shorter supply chains to enhance profits and sustainability for small growers.[8] Supply chains are changing and shortening in virtually every industry worldwide thanks to the global marketplace created by the Internet, and it's realistic to believe they will continue to do so.

'Supply chains that are agile by reacting speedily to changes in demand or supply and adapt overtime as market structure and strategies evolve and those that align the interest of all firms in the supply network so that companies optimise the chains performance are the ones that gain a sustainable competitive advantage'.[9]

Here's an example of the ultimate vertical supply chain model. In 1995, the iconic Idaho potato farmer billionaire J.R. Simplot purchased Edgell Australia along with its portfolio of brands including Leggo's, Nanna's, Four n Twenty and Birdseye. He had made his fortune in the 1970s by supplying McDonald's with 50% of their frozen French fries in the US. Simplot owned the land the potatoes were grown on, the farm machinery, the fertilizer company and the logistics company that shipped them. The question is how can you incorporate a small part of this vertical model to shorten your supply chain?

Becoming part of a buying group or franchise may be one answer and sourcing a portion of your stock through a shorter supply chain may be another. Independent paint shops can already purchase accessories direct from manufacturers and side step higher priced national suppliers. Independent music stores can buy guitar strings and capos online from US manufactured brands and source guitars direct from Chinese factories cheaper than national wholesalers can supply them today. Many specialty retailers across many industry segments already import direct from factories in Asia to shorten their chain of supply and improve their competitiveness.

The changing supply chain is problematic for the future of precariously placed middlemen in danger of becoming irrelevant. The changing supply chain is a challenge that many specialty retailers and their suppliers are trying desperately to ignore but nevertheless will face as a matter of urgency in the coming years. The changing supply chain means those retailers who build direct supply into some or all of their purchasing will grow and prosper with sustainable margins and competitive pricing to the end user for years to come.

Secret 3-Know your customers

Listening to your customers is an essential part of best practice in business generally. Short surveys, small gifts in exchange for feedback and simple conversations all provide mechanisms to allow communication flow in order for you to know **who your customers are**, what they want and how they shop.

Today's consumer is changing and the Internet has certainly impacted how your customers shop and what they buy. It seems that the online shopping channel is not going away and so there's little point ignoring the numbers as they continue to grow.

According to the Australian National Retailers Association (ANRA), Australians spent AUD $32.7 billion in the lead up to Christmas 2012 and $6.9 billion, nearly 20 percent, was spent online.[10] $2.6 billion of that was spent with offshore or overseas retailers. Boxing-day 2012 showed the Myer.com.au website recording a stunning 5000 online sales. In August 2012, the Australian Bureau of Statistics reported that online shopping in Australia represented 6% of overall sales. The UK equivalent was 13.5% and the United States was 8%. More recent figures from NAB online retail sales index in the year to July 2013 reported that online spending amounted to $14.1billion or 6.3% of traditional retail sales.[11] Australia's postal service reported an increase in parcels of 13% in the year to June 2013 and directly attributes growth to online retail sales.

In one year, the value of the online retail market grew by $2 billion. It is now worth $13.1 billion.[12] Finn Haensel from the website iconic.com.au predicts that share will grow to 30-40% within 4 years![13] Whether you believe him or not, these statistics are directly impacting on your business and are as undeniable as the science of global warming.

The rapid move toward online shopping combined with changes in the structure of populations or demographics such as age, sex, lifestyle and diversity are adding to the gradual deterioration of the traditional bricks and mortar retail model worldwide.

For example, in 2013 the Myer Centre in Brisbane's CBD reported that 60% of shoppers were female. Another significant change was that 25% of all shoppers were from Asian backgrounds. It is important to consider how this information would impact you if you had a 5-year lease in that shopping centre. What is the population demographic in your area and how can you adapt your business model to connect with the changing consumer and their buying choices to regain relevance and capture growth?

If you do not have an online presence and rely solely on the bricks and mortar income stream, it's time you consider joining market leaders with a business to consumer (B2C) website and social networking sites (SNS) that are relevant to your new customers enabling them to buy 24/7 and stay in touch with your retail brand.

'Demographic targeting is the key to success when it comes to modern retailing. The retailer who ignores the demographics of his customers does so at his own peril'.[14]

Knowing and understanding your customer demographic or target markets, what they want and how they shop is primarily and vitally important to all of the marketing and rebranding elements discussed in **Retail Rebranded.**

Secret 4-Incorporate sustainability

A snapshot of our planet shows that humans currently operate at 140% of its resources. The United Nations predicts that between 2035 and 2050 we will need two planets to support natural resource consumption and absorption of the waste we produce.[15] According to the World Wildlife Fund, the really bad news is that if everyone in the world consumed like Aussies, the global population would need 3.76 planets to support it[16] and I don't believe they are ready for men on Mars and women on Venus just yet!

Professor Jorgen Randers, a Norwegian climate change expert has been studying unsustainable global practices and trying to change Government mindsets for 40 years. His concern is that our grandchildren are headed for a train wreck. A two degrees global temperature increase by 2050 and three degrees by 2080 is predicted, leading to widespread environmental, social and economic collapse.[17] Our way of living is simply not sustainable no matter how you look at it.

As 2013 signals the 37th consecutive year of global temperature increases,[18] it is obvious that not only on a macro (large) scale but also a micro (small) scale, we all need to do our bit if we are to slow the impacts of global warming and the poisoning of our planet's environment by further CO^2 emissions.

Professor Randers suggests that the developed countries of the world need to lead the way with green energy alternatives because developing countries simply cannot afford these innovations. Even though Australia, for example, fits this bill, we still dig up dirty fuel resources such as coal and uranium and ship it off to our neighbouring developing countries to fuel their rise into the middle class, so they too can live beyond their means and accelerate the planet's pollution into the latter part of this century.

With some of the world's largest economies already on the brink of financial Armageddon, climate change gaining momentum and technology playing an ever growing part in society, change in how we live and consume is being forced upon us at a rapid rate never before seen. We have no choice, we must change and adapt or fail and perish and so with it must the framework of sustainable living, manufacturing and retailing.

The National Retail Association (NRA) advocates for sustainability practices in Australia and lists four objectives in their sustainability charter. Energy and greenhouse gas emissions, water, waste and recycling and communicating, reporting and engaging.[19]

In addition, a report from the Retail Industry Leaders Association (RILA) in the United States indicates that sustainability is 'becoming a core consideration for the retail industry, affecting strategy, operations, workforce engagement and connection to consumers and communities'.[20] This report outlines four key retail sustainability factors including working across sectors to achieve sustainability goals, turning from sustainability as a cost and risk reduction measure to an opportunity for business growth, developing systems for continuous improvement and fostering transparency in operations and the supply chain. It affirms integration, relationships, collaboration and RBM improvement as representative of future retail industry direction. The benefits of sustainability outlined to all stakeholders include improved efficiencies, risk mitigation, sourcing of new innovations, recruitment and retention of top talent, entry to new geographies and product markets and improved reputation.

The European Retail Round Table also focuses on sustainable retailing as the 'backbone of business'.[21] All of these reports from every corner of the developed world clearly agree that sustainability is increasingly important to the retail sector and must be embraced now.

In the Australian manufacturing sector, global competitiveness is undeniably a key driver towards economic growth and sustainability. The Australian treasurer, the Hon. Joe Hockey MP, passionately believes that the manufacturing sector needs reinvention and agrees that digging up dirty fuel resources for export is unsustainable. In the treasurer's own words: 'It's an hypocrisy'.[22]

Listening to him address an audience recently, it hit home to me that three generations of my own family relied on Australian manufacturing for our 'fair go' and all the opportunities my parents gave us came from making Holden motor cars and Levi jeans from factories that are now closed due to uncompetitive and unsustainable practices.

The challenge now for Australian manufacturers and many other western nations is to 'redefine themselves and seize the opportunity of innovation and harness emerging technologies to develop new and sustainable ways to remain competitive'.[23] There's no doubt that Australian manufacturing needs resurrection because lack of global competitiveness is impacting on the retail supply chain, retail competitiveness and retail sustainability.

Poor economic conditions, the growing Internet monster, unwillingness to change, the absence of sustainability and innovation, climate change, escalating overheads, increases to superannuation, penalty rates and the resulting inability to compete, all impact to tell a gloomy story for two million small businesses and five million employees that are the lifeblood of the Australian economy.

Whilst I do believe many more retailers will collapse, I truly believe the remaining retailscape will demonstrate a remarkably higher overall standard that embraces dynamic change and bases decision making on sustainability, innovation, competitiveness and best practice in every facet of relevant contemporary retailing.

We know that your competitors are no longer just local or domestic and we know that you operate in a global village where consumerism is a simple click, pat of the mouse pad, or a Google glass[24] away. Compared to the new global benchmark in retail, many specialty retailers have much work to do to regain their competitiveness by incorporating sustainability elements into their RBM.

Leading the way by offering consumers unique and distinctive brand experiences through competitive and sustainable business models are global retailers Apple, Nespresso, Starbucks and Zara. These retailers have adopted diverse, flexible, experiential and vertical models. Woolworths, Coles, IKEA and the Body Shop stand amongst countless success stories that never sit still and continuously strive to improve their RBM. These brands have all emerged as 'brick n click' retailers with models that are sustainable for them and their customers.

Way back in 1997, the dark ages it seems, internationally renowned 'dean of corporate responsibility' and sustainability expert, John Elkington coined the term 'triple bottom line'. It refers to the sustainability of profit, people and the planet.[25] In other words, it refers to how economic sustainability, social sustainability and environmental sustainability affect your bottom line.

Have you ever really thought about sustainability in terms of profit, people and the planet and what the real implications are for your business? Have you ever asked yourself what your unique proposition that differentiates your brand from the rest is? Now is the time.

As environmental sustainability becomes more of a pressing issue for younger generations, sustainable products and retail brands that advocate for sustainability will gain in popularity. As generations Y and younger align their sense of wanting to help the environment through personal micro shopping choices, they will also prefer to work in socially sustainable environments for employers who have built long-term economic sustainability into their retail branding.

Sustainability practices will continue to be further integrated into branding, marketing, business, manufacturing and retail. It will become more fashionable and indeed necessary as business realises and builds-in the cost benefits of sustainability. I believe that retailers who stock environmentally friendly products, align with eco suppliers and enhance the consumer's ability to minimise waste and energy usage will become the retail brands of choice.

Ultimately, the challenge for specialty retailers is to offer sustainability as an integrated part of the consumer brand experience on every level possible.[26] That means including sustainability as a core brand value or ethic and the ability to communicate that to customers and target audiences will become increasingly important.

If you choose to incorporate sustainability dimensions into your retail branding, you can add strength to your position by using suppliers that also incorporate environmental, social and economic sustainability into their business models. This is particularly relevant to food retailing where organic, local and ethically sourced food is gaining a higher profile and can potentially add to your 'brand equity' or value.

Incorporating sustainability into your brand's core values will provide a clear and contemporary platform to reassess, reposition, rename, redesign and relaunch your retail brand. The challenge is to look at ways to incorporate sustainability through innovation to front-of-house and back-end operations to enhance your profitability, your people and your planet and with it, the capacity to endure into the future.

Secret 5-Innovate

'Innovation is a key driver of brand growth'.[27] Applied in your business context, it is defined as a change beyond current practice in one or more elements of an RBM i.e. retailing format, activities and governance.[28]

Research on innovation clearly indicates that innovative practices can enhance the consumers overall shopping experience and improve retailer brand equity.[29] Innovations in business models are increasingly critical for building sustainable advantage in a marketplace defined by unrelenting change, escalating customer expectations, and intense competition.[30] An added bonus is that innovation can also enhance your sustainability and can be applied to all aspects of your RBM not just with regard to new technologies.

There are six major ways retailers can apply innovation to their RBM to enhance value. They are operational efficiency and effectiveness, customer lock-in, customer efficiency, customer effectiveness and customer engagement. Here are examples of how to incorporate innovation into your RBM from the recent 2011 work of academics in the United States and The Netherlands.[31] I have added some example retailers that you may be familiar with.

Applying Innovation to your RBM

Application of	What?	How?
Operational efficiency	Incorporate best practice to back-end Become faster, cheaper, simpler	Reduce assortment Manage inventory levels for fast turnaround or stock turns. **Zara** Enhance store environments through optimisation of layouts, category, shelf management and self-service to maximise returns. **Bunnings, Masters** Automate processes **Walmart** Minimise waste
Operational effectiveness	Incorporate adjacency model	Capitalise on adjacent demand by expanding outside the boundaries of the business. **IKEA** Maximise organisational objectives Understand your target markets Understand your customers needs Offer products tied-in with services and company knowledge **Apple**
Customer lock-in	Capture repeat business through customer loyalty Leveraging exclusive products	Offer a unique product assortment Introduce subtle loyalty programs Create enduring customer relationships Incorporate private label brands at lower prices **Target, Aldi**

Application of	What?	How?
Customer efficiency	Make customer access to products as easy as possible Improve the overall shopping experience (OSE)	Dual placement merchandising strategies Applying the store-within-a-store concept Selling in multiple channels (instore-online-mobile) Selling across channels (Buy online pick up in-store) **McDonald's inside Masters, Dan Murphy, Woolworths**
Customer effectiveness	Work with suppliers to determine optimal assortment Customer co-creation where customers and retailers collaborate to create consumer products	Add e-tail (B2C website) to RBM to expand range online Introduce personalisation of products where possible **M&M's, Amazon, Nike, Nespresso, Birdsnest**
Customer engagement Become retailer of choice Sell brand ideology Incorporate sustainability as a core value Add value to your offer		Design customer experiences that evoke emotional involvement through store design Selling products that sustain people and the planet **Body Shop, Walmart, IKEA**

Trust the French!

Mark, a Gen-Y from New Caledonia, told me his father had a small supermarket where cruise ships stop and up to 2000 people walked past and into their store on any given day, yet the business was not doing well. His father couldn't understand why sales conversions were so poor. Mark came up with the suggestion to his dad of showing the prices in multiple currencies to their customers and taking any foreign currency for payment on any items. This meant that customers could easily understand the store's value proposition in their own currency. Mark's father looked into how they could implement this change and discovered he could install a digital price label system that hooked up to a central computer for easy, fast and efficient price changes when necessary. The prices could be rotated in multiple currencies on each individual price ticket that was mounted on the front of shelving units. The system came at a cost but Mark's father took the risk and installed it. Sales went through the roof and tourists were happy to buy all manner of things to save them money on the cruise ship. This innovation saved the family business. **Technological innovation improves your business model**

Secret 6-Go online

The Internet represents the single largest innovation in modern history and e-tail has changed re-tail forever. The state of play for online retailing in Australia has been outlined in a 2010 report from Korda Mentha.[32] It suggests that based on credit and debit card transactions, the Commonwealth Bank estimates that online transactions represented AUD$10 billion with AUD$4 billion being spent with overseas retailers.

US retailers have been particularly good at focusing on the Australian marketplace to poach new customers. Sales to Australia now represent one third of the USA's total overseas sales and growing. Incidentally, 25% of online buyers were aged 25-34 years old and 32% of all sales were from multi-category retailers (i.e. Amazon and Walmart).

The report also suggests that the lack of online presence before 2011 by major Australian retailers is to blame for a 3-5 year lag behind the United States and the United Kingdom. This lag has been compounded not only by retailers wasting time lobbying Government to lower the $1000 import threshold but also by late adoption and support from management to incorporate online as a new part of the RBM. The Australian productivity commission found that the uncompetitiveness of Aussie retailers was more influenced by high rent and wage conditions than it was by the 10% GST on goods.

Online Australian retailers have been uncompetitive by more than just the 10% represented by the GST and have been slow to create an effective online sales platform. For the largest retailers in Australia, the move online was a reluctant one but one that now, some years later, is beginning to return rewards. **Going online** is unmistakably essential for the success of your retail rebranding no matter where you are in the world.

The next paradigm shift in consumer purchase behaviour is expected to be through the mobile commerce (m-commerce) channel or smart phone technology. Unfortunately, the Korda Mentha report states that Australian retailers were slow to innovate and lacked imagination despite 25% of Australians in 2010 purchasing goods online from mobile devices. The good news is that 34,000 small businesses are transacting online with Pay Pal and are experiencing growth. These businesses are growing in part because of their inclusion of the online element to their RBM.

One example of a large Australian retailer that now incorporates the m-commerce channel is Dan Murphy. The liquor e-tailer is one of many that have successfully combined its traditional paper catalogue with smart phone technology. When consumers download the Dan Murphy iPhone application they are able to photograph the products in the catalogue they wish to purchase and ordering, payment and delivery options are made easy!

In the pages that follow, we will look at many ways to incorporate sustainability through innovation and you will discover your own way to improve your retail business in your own context. Those retailers who are willing to innovate and experiment with ongoing evolutionary changes will find themselves in the best position to realise growth now and into the future.

What is rebranding?

Rebranding means updating the *image* of your organisation to external stakeholders such as customers and suppliers and changing the *identity* of your brand to internal stakeholders such as owners and staff. Rebranding aims to differentiate brand positioning in the minds of all stakeholders and to create a distinctive identity from your competitors.[33]

My work in this book on retail rebranding can be explained as a combination of two and a half decades of my own experience with academic research from around the globe. I have worked at the coalface in retail as a salesperson, manager, merchandiser, wholesaler, trainer, motivational speaker and retail consultant to businesses just like yours across Australia and travelled widely in Asia and the Americas researching best practice in many retail segments.

Marketing academics have carried out research around *corporate* rebranding. For example, Professor Mary Lambkin, Dr. Laurent Muzallec and Manus Doogan from the University of Dublin defined four steps to corporate rebranding in their 2003 work.[34] Professor Bill Merrilees and Dr. Dale Miller from Griffith University, Gold Coast campus, outlined the principles of corporate rebranding in their 2008 research.[35] I have combined their research and more with my experience and added the extra step of 'reassess' to formulate the new and contemporary five-step process I call **Retail Rebranding**.

There are definite similarities between corporate and retail branding environments. Market leading retailers use a corporate strategy and vision for their brands. Many specialty retailers refer to their market leading competitors as 'the corporates'. Those corporate retailers and online sellers make up the retail brand landscape or *brandscape* that exists around you.

There are three elements of corporate branding that can be applied to retail branding and must align to achieve greatness. They are vision, culture and image.[36] Your retail brand vision must come from the top and it must come from you in an enthusiastic and inspirational way. Great vision always comes from great leaders and the biggest retail brands in the world were born from individuals with a great brand vision. Your retail brand culture is the values, behaviours and attitudes that you develop in all employees in your organisation. Your retail brand image is everybody else's overall impression of your brand. This includes all other stakeholders such as customers, shareholders, the media, suppliers and the general public. All these factors must align in order to get the best result from your overall branding strategy and build equity for your retail brand.

The biggest advantage of being a specialty retailer over a corporate retailer is that you have the ability to make changes quickly. Retail rebranding can provide the platform to help you enter more aggressive markets and face more aggressive competitors *and fast!*

Before I let you in on more of the secrets that market leaders don't really want you to know, let's first highlight that the opportunity to incorporate changes in your business relies openly and objectively with you.

Secret 7-Put your BIG on!

One way to recognise the latest trends in the global village in which you now operate and stay on top of what your competitors are doing, is to look closely at the retailscape and the brandscape around you. There are a number of things you can do to inform yourself and get your own sense of what is happening in your local area, across the country and around the world.

It is very useful to develop what I call your business intelligence goggles or 'BIG'. This is where you scan your environment to pick up helpful information that can be applied to your own business. Learning to think BIG is important to help you introduce new ideas and practices into your RBM. Here are some ways that you can develop your objective and open thinking, so *put your BIG on* to gain a new perspective that will help you capture the competitive advantage that sets you apart from the rest.

- **Develop** observational checklists for the different areas of your business i.e. staff performance, merchandising, housekeeping, customer service, operations etc. This will help to identify any efficiency gaps you may have when comparing to your market leading competitors.
- **Read** relevant trade magazines and subscribe to informational websites and blogs to get up-to-date information on latest trends in the marketplace. *Google it!*
- **Join** retail associations in your region to gain access to information and services. [37]
- **Observe** what your competitors are doing by visiting their stores regularly. Check out their websites and mobile apps, compare prices, note changes in layouts

or merchandising strategies, watch their promotions and observe customer behaviour and response.

- **Apply** the elements into your own business that you discover through observational research. This is known as R n D or 'Rip off and Duplicate!'[38]

- **Visit** your market or category leaders and new entrant stores regularly to see what they are implementing in terms of location, layout, store design, merchandise assortment, visual merchandising, pricing, promotions and service standards. If you think BIG, this exercise can help you refine and differentiate your brand to enhance your uniqueness and desirability to the consumer.

- **Listen** to and use your resources (employees and family) as they represent the future of your business and are often in touch with today's technology and how their peers think, network and shop. Ask for staff input and listen to their suggestions. They will feel valued and you will get the information you need to regain or retain relevance in your marketplace.

- **Experience** your store as a first time new customer. If you find it difficult to be objective, send in a friend to 'mystery shop' your store for an honest opinion about your overall brand experience and how it stacks up against your competitors.

- **Ask** your customers to give you honest feedback through personal conversations and communication mechanisms such as questionnaires or small rewards for feedback.

All these methods can help open your mind and your ability to change, which are essential elements towards personal and business growth. I am sure all these verbs or 'doing words' have inspired you to **put your BIG on**, take a good look around and start your to-do list! The next question I can hear you asking is...

Why rebrand?

There are many reasons you might be considering rebranding as a vehicle towards growth:

- Under performance.[39] *Your business has slumped and you are not happy with your sales.*
- Merger or acquisition.[40] *You purchased a store and you need to choose a single brand to merge multiple stores.*
- Modernise or revamp your image.[41] *You feel like you are outdated and you wish to appeal to new target segments.*
- Changes in external environment.[42] *You have a new entrant or player in your category and you think you may have lost your competitive advantage.*
- Increase brand equity/awareness. *Your brand does not have recognition factor and you are being ignored or becoming irrelevant to your target segments.*
- Help the brand expand domestically/globally. *You want to expand interstate or overseas.*
- Reassociate the brand with the main product or service. *Your brand no longer aligns with what you sell and is not aligned with your core values or ethics.*
- Achieve contemporary relevance.[43] *Your brand is perceived as old or tired and it's time to update it.*

One or more of these reasons may resonate with you in some way. In my experience, many specialty retailers are underperforming and are unhappy with the way their business is tracking. If you haven't updated the image of your retail brand for four or more years, it's time to rebrand and refresh now anyway.

Let's get to it and begin by asking this very important and sometimes confronting question: **Is your retail brand effective?**

This is where you need to be brutally honest with yourself and take the test. If you don't know the answers, think BIG and use your observational research skills to look around you closely and objectively to *find* the answers.

Ask your customers and employees what they think and feel about your brand and be open to constructive and not-so-constructive criticisms. Answer 'Yes' or 'No' in the table below and fill in the blanks for a clearer picture of how your brand may be perceived.

Is your retail brand effective?

The following is a short quiz that I have adapted from research to help you find out if you have an effective retail brand. [44]

- Does your current brand **name** differentiate your product/service positively from other, similar offers in the marketplace in the mind of the customer? Y/N
- Is your brand differentiated and a unique experience? Is it memorable? Y/N
- Do you or your management have sufficient control to guarantee a reliable customer experience **everytime**? Y/N
- Can your brand attract customers from further away than your competing retailers? Y/N
- Do customers spend longer in your store than in similar stores? Y/N

My competitor/s brands	Differences they are:	Differences we are:	Objective feedback from staff/customers
1.			
2.			
3.			

If you answered 'No' to two or more questions then it's possible some or all of the following conditions exist for your retail store brand:

- Your customers perceive there is no inherent quality in your products.
- Your brand represents an undifferentiated experience and is similar to many other retail offers.
- Your products are sold at a discount under other products in similar stores and do not or cannot sell at a premium.
- Your products and retail brand attract local customers only.
- Customers spend as little time as possible in the store and do not enjoy browsing.
- Management control is insufficient to provide a reliable experience every time.
- Does your current brand command a higher or premium price than your competitors for similar products or service because of an image for quality and/or reliability? Y/N
- Are your **products** differentiated and unique? Y/N

My competitor/s products	Differences they have:	Differences we have:	Objective feedback from staff/customers
1.			
2.			
3.			

- Can your brand be valued, used, sold or licensed separately from the business owning the brand/name? This is called a 'separate existence' and relates to brand equity. Y/N
- Is your brand name capable of transfer to other products or services for the purpose of brand extension or diversification? Y/N

Is it possible that your brand is of little or no value on other services or products? Y/N

- Does your brand offer benefits to the customer at a symbolic or sensory level? This is called 'emotional or psychic value'. Y/N

An example of a symbolic benefit might be that consumers buy handbags so people can see they paid a lot of money i.e. Louis Vuitton or Hermes. Symbolic purchasing is very prevalent in some cultures. This can be the case for boutique or specialty retail brands that may be part of a pop culture or relevant to a particular demographic. An example of a sensory benefit might be the product/brand smells nice and customers can try it in-store i.e. The Body Shop or similar specialty retailer.

- Do purchases from your retail brand enhance the self-image of customers? Y/N
- Does the process of buying (browsing, service, environment, packaging) enhance the self-image of customers? Y/N

List of Benefits to my customers	Sensory level benefits (touch, see, feel, hear)	Psychic level benefits (emotional response) i.e. 'I love the bags they package their products in)
1.		
2.		
3.		

Is it possible that the following is true for your brand?

- Purchases do not enhance the customer's self-image.

- The buying process alienates the customer at times. An example of this could be that you do not have prices on all your goods and therefore customers are forced to ask when they don't want to.

You should now have a clearer picture of how your brand is perceived by your customers or at least identified that you may need some reshaping. It is not an easy task to remain objective about your own retail brand and how your customers may or may not perceive it to be. *Well done for answering some tricky questions!*

Secret 8- Get a brand personality

How you want your refreshed brand to be perceived by your target segments and especially new target segments should be carefully considered. This perception can be enhanced to build your brand equity if you understand what your brand's personality is or what you want it to be.

American Professor of Marketing and Social Psychologist Dr. Jennifer Aaker from Stanford University, suggests there are five major personality dimensions for brands.[45] I have added retail brands from around the world.

1. **Sincerity** (domestic, honest, genuine and cheerful) e.g. Terry White Chemist, Specsavers, Macy's, Ralph Lauren
2. **Excitement** (daring, spirited, imaginative and up-to-date) e.g. Apple, Sportsgirl, IKEA, Guess, American Apparel
3. **Competence** (reliable, responsible, dependable and efficient) e.g. David Jones, Myer, Macy's, Harrods
4. **Sophistication** (glamorous, pretentious, charming and romantic) e.g. Michael Hill, Zara, Hermes, H&M
5. **Ruggedness** (tough, strong, outdoorsy and rugged) e.g. Kathmandu, Rebel Sport, Nike

Think about which one or combinations of these you wish to project to your customers. Decide which ones fit with you and your brand vision. Interestingly, Dr. Aaker suggests that the symbolic use of brands is different across cultures. For example, in cultures where independence, autonomy and uniqueness are valued i.e. western culture, consumers are more likely to buy brands to express how they differ from their 'in-group'. Conversely, in cultures that value interdependence, conformity and similarity i.e. eastern cultures, consumers are more likely to buy brands that express their similarities to their in-group.

This information is highly relevant in today's marketplace where there is a mixture of eastern and western cultures. *How?* It may impact your target markets and how they perceive and connect with your retail brand. It may also affect your choice of product brands and the stock quantities that you purchase.

It is possible that you have never thought about your store in terms of a brand with a personality before. Your competitors certainly consider themselves as retail brands with personality and image, so you can feel completely justified that you too can be a retail brand that has a personality and an image, just like you have your own personal brand, personality and image. At the end of each section, I provide you with some quick tips that summarise what we have covered in each step of retail rebranding.

Quick Tips to step 1 reassess

1. **Conduct** your SWOT analysis and plan for new revenue streams
2. **Consider** your supply chain and diversify it where possible
3. **Think** about who your customers are, what they want and how they shop
4. **Open** your mind to the idea of applying sustainability to profit, people and the planet
5. **Begin** to think of ways you can apply changes to your RBM through innovation
6. **Think** BIG and observe your competitors closely
7. **Understand** why you need to rebrand
8. **Take** the test to see if you have an effective brand
9. **Choose** your personality type or a combination
10. **Compile** some notes and begin your to-do list

2-reposition

Secret 9-Know who you are

When repositioning your retail brand it is critical to think about who you really are. Remember the definition of branding is *who you are* and *what you do*. Ask yourself what are your brand values or what is the *soul* of your company? For example, part of IKEA's core brand values statement is to 'create an everyday better life for the many people'.[46] This statement outlines that IKEA stands for making a difference in peoples lives through social sustainability.

Examine what core values your brand currently projects to your customers and then look at your competitors. It's important to gain an understanding about how you fit into the brandscape around you and how you would like to reposition your brand using your core values as a guide.

Your core values are connected with the overall mindset and culture within your organisation and cannot be stronger externally than internally. That is, the internal values of your retail brand, held by management and staff, need to resonate with the values *perceived* by your customers and other external stakeholders.

Associate Professor Dr. Mats Urde from Sweden's Lund University says that core values can evolve over time and must be constantly monitored to ensure you have not strayed from what you really stand for. Professor Urde concludes that if you are to have credible core brand values, you must live up to them day-by-day and customer-by-customer.[47]

For example, if your core values statement is 'to provide stellar customer satisfaction through efficient, innovative and sustainable products and practices' you must be able to guarantee customer satisfaction every time and present innovative and sustainable products every time. Can you do that? Is it a reasonable, feasible and believable expectation of your brand? If so, then you and your staff must fight to exemplify your brand core values and hold fast when they are tested or challenged. Believe in them resolutely. The strength of your brand is of course determined by the promise you make and the promises you keep!

To help you achieve your brand promise, you could incorporate a minimum service standard that every single customer experiences when entering your store that is designed upon efficiency, innovation and sustainability. You could outline the service standard to your people and measure outcomes. Your team could practice delivering it every time to every customer in every possible way in order to uphold your core brand values.

It is important that your core brand values statement is based on connecting with your customers and your *new target customers* in order to gain value from any rebranding updates you make. After all, attracting new customer segments to your brand may be part of your reason to embark on a rebranding journey in the first place. Think about your brand meaning to your new customers. How will it be perceived? What should you change about it? Why are you in business and what is meaningful about what you do?

The first thing you learn when you go to business school is that you are in business to make money. Obviously, economic sustainability is the reason everyone is in business, but is it a core brand value? Why else are you in business? Are there social or environmental reasons that you can incorporate? If so, integrate them into your core values and tell your customers, employees and suppliers what they are and what they mean to them, in their lives.

Here is a list[48] of values and some retail examples of applied values. Simply circle the values that stand out to you and then eliminate them until you have three or four left. These remaining values are the ones you would most likely use in your core values statement. Be sure to align your core values with your brand personality and always keep your new customers in mind.

Core values table

Accuracy	Achievement	Acknowledgement	Alertness	Assertiveness
Brilliance	Community **Vinnies**	Carefulness	Cheerfulness	Commitment
Compassion	Competence	Connection	Conservation	Consistency
Contribution **Apple**	Conviction	Daring **Victoria's secret**	Dependability	Determination
Devotion	Diversity	Effectiveness	Efficiency	Energy **Boost Juice**
Environmentalism **The Body Shop**	Ethics **Starbucks**	Excellence **Louis Vuitton**	Excitement	Exhilaration
Experience	Expertise	Faith	Family **IKEA**	Fun
Growth	Happiness	Health **Boots**	Honesty	Humor
Imagination	Individuality **Ed Hardy**	Integrity **Urban Outfitters**	Innovation **Apple**	Knowledge
Leadership	Longevity **Harrods**	Love	Meaning	Philanthropy
Relaxation	Reliability **Bloomingdale's**	Reputation **Tiffany & Co.**	Respect	Responsibility
Satisfaction **IKEA**	Service	Sincerity	Sophistication **Nespresso**	Strength **Adidas**
Teamwork	Trust **Macy's**	Uniqueness	Variety **Walgreens**	Zeal **H&M**

The Starbucks brand is an example synonymous with ethical and sustainable sourcing of coffee beans and it has developed a standard for business conduct for all areas of its business model. Its core values statement that follows, outlines Starbucks as:

'The premier purveyor of the finest coffee in the world while maintaining uncompromising principles as we grow. Providing a great work environment and treating each other with respect and dignity. Embracing diversity as an essential component in the way we do business. Applying the highest standards of excellence to the purchasing, roasting and fresh delivery of our coffee. Developing enthusiastically satisfied customers all of the time and contributing positively to our communities and our environment and to recognize that profitability is essential to our future success'. [49]

This core values statement may be lengthy but it leaves no doubt with the consumer, employee or supplier what the brand stands for. Your statement can be as long or short as you like. Use a pencil to write below, as you may like to modify your core values statement later on.

_____

_____

_____

_____

Take some time to think about it to make sure your core values fit with the overall vision you have for your revised brand. Once you have settled on your core values, ask yourself again how to align your statement with your suppliers. For example, there's little point espousing that you are a socially sustainable brand if you stock products sourced through unfair trade in Asia or Africa. If you are doing that, it makes sense not to mention socially aware brand statements in your rebranding communications.

Can you recall a few years ago when a major sporting brand was in the media for unethical manufacture of their footwear? The negative press affected their overall brand equity or brand value and it was a short-term revenue disaster for the product brand. Think carefully about what your brand *is* and what it *stands for.*

Secret 10-Know your competitors

When was the last time you visited your competitors? Some specialty retailers tell me they are not in competition with anyone. Actually, your competitors may not be immediately obvious to you unless you think BIG and take a closer look around. For example, if you sell recreational products like musical instruments, your indirect competitor is a computer game reseller in your precinct or online. You are competing for the same dollar, from the same target market. Therefore, you are in competition.

Another example could be that you are an independent jeweller in a community shopping centre or mall. You have two brands directly competing against you and one is the market leader. Where are you positioned? Are you more exclusive and higher priced than Pandora, lower priced and more affordable than K-Mart, or in between? Are you upscale or downscale from these competitors or line-ball? What product brands do you stock and how does that affect your positioning? Where do the opportunities for growth lie?

You must know where you sit in your brand positioning in order to clarify your retail concept so you can work out your target segments and where to reposition. You may believe you have higher customer service standards and a superior in-store experience than your competitors, but is that really the case? Have you experienced your competitors' customer service first hand and compared it objectively with your own?

Have you asked your customers who is better, you or them? How does your pricing compare to theirs? What about your location? Do your store layout, signage, design and visual merchandising standards scrub up? Are your window displays effective? Is your product assortment still relevant? Are your promotions timely, competitive and well executed?

All these retail 'mix' factors require thorough investigation before you consider where you will **reposition** your brand against your competitors so you can reposition where there is the most opportunity for growth. If you are already a market leader, it is essential that your brand does not become complacent over time and that you continue to change and update your brand to remain relevant to your target markets and changing customer segments.

In my view, there is a major Australian airline, albeit a service brand, that has exemplified complacency. As market leader in business travel for decades, the airline has clearly been struggling to update its domestic branding and maintain its position as market leader.

As a result, brand equity may have been damaged through it being perceived as tired, ageing and heading towards irrelevance to some segments of its market. I once experienced a flight to Honolulu with the airline in an old clapped out aeroplane that was too small for long haul and in need of new seats and a new staff attitude! The airline lounge was tired and too small for the demand and so was forced to turn people away, further damaging its reputation and brand equity. The experience completely changed my perception of the airline overnight and I went from loyal to unsatisfied and began looking at its competitors for options.

Another airline has taken the top spot in the Australian business travel market due to its recent rebranding activities and improvements to its business model. The rebranding program was carefully planned and executed by the organisation soon after a new CEO was appointed. The rebranding strategy saw this airline take the lead through updates to all brand interactions or 'touchpoints' such as aircraft, lounges, loyalty programs, logos, colours, staff uniforms, check-in counters, signage and service standards.

This refresh saw profits soar whilst the opposition recorded it's worst full-year loss since records began in 1953.[50] The floundering airline attempted to sustain its position by moving aircraft maintenance off shore to cut costs. Meanwhile, in my experience, service standards declined and many aircraft, lounges and staff became stale and with it, the overall brand experience.

These two global and domestic airlines remain acutely aware of each other's activities in the marketplace. They constantly monitor and even head hunt executives and personnel in order to gain insight into their competitor's activities. In late January 2014, I noticed that the once complacent airline started to communicate through billboard advertising that it has embarked on a rebranding update. Interesting! It will be interesting to watch what now unfolds in the airline sector! Checking your competitors to observe and understand their activities is vital in order to reposition and compete effectively.

Know thine enemy

Having worked with many hundreds of specialty retailers, I ask many of them when they last visited their competitors stores. They invariably answer with 'I never go in there, they are the enemy!' **If you don't get out and check out your competitors how can you truly compete?**

You stand to make enormous gains by watching your market leading competitors closely. When you carry out a reconnaissance mission or 'recci' of your competitors, the aim is to gain knowledge about some of their costly resources such as research, marketing, merchandising, HR, operations, management and innovations. Then you can incorporate their 'best practices' into your small to medium enterprise to improve your RBM. Conduct R'n'D; *'Rip-off and duplicate'!* [51]

Find out what your competitors market share is. Often this information is publicly available online through reports to industry or shareholders. Work out what your market share is or could be. This exercise highlights more opportunities for *you*. What your leading competitors are doing more than likely represents current best practice in your category or segment, so venture into their stores thinking BIG to look, listen and learn about how they run their business, *what they do* and *how they do it.*

A simple example is, let's say your competitor is a department store that's best practice standard is to merchandise homewares via the colour blocking method. You could use that same tactic of arranging merchandise together in your store by colour group to produce a visually effective strategy that sells more merchandise.

It may take some effort on your behalf or perhaps investment to hire a professional merchandiser, but what do you have to lose? If the department store merchandises by pricepoint around the store during a sale period, try that tactic to see if it works for you too. There is only knowledge, insight and market share to be gained by incorporating new practices into your business that market leaders already employ.

Secret 11-Position your brand clearly

Repositioning your brand aims to create a new position in the minds of your customers, competitors and other stakeholders. Brand positioning is a dynamic and gradual process, which must be adjusted regularly to stay in tune with shifting market trends, competitor positioning and the changing consumer.[52]

Highlighting your points-of-parity (sameness) and points-of-difference (uniqueness) with those of your competitors will help you understand where you are currently positioned so you can reposition in order to capitalise on market opportunities. It is unlikely that you have no competitors in your business category, so begin by looking at who they are and figuring out what they do and how they do it. Look at what you sell and then look at all others who sell the same or similar products. This will help you create or highlight unique retail brand attributes adding up to a brand personality that will help you stand out from the crowd. Here's an example.

Competitor comparison

Brand	Target market	Points of Difference (POD)	Points of Parity (POP)	Pricing
Loot	Female under 35	Everyday low prices (EDLP) Cluttered merchandising Sell online	Similar logo colours to 'HighEnd'	Cheapest
Myer or Macy's	High end female 25-60	Well merchandised Sell online	Maxwell and Williams	Mid range

Brand	Target market	Points of Difference (POD)	Points of Parity (POP)	Pricing
'HighEnd Homewares' (you)	Specialty, all customer ages	Offer service and exclusive brands, nicer store fit out and lighting. Boutique brands Excellent merchandising Don't sell online	Maxwell and Williams	Premium price

This table shows an example of your positioning above your competitors with regard to quality, pricing and perceived value. The idea is to make your positioning very clear to your customers through all elements of your **retail mix** which includes store location, layout, design, merchandise assortment, visual merchandising, pricing, promotions and customer service.[53]

If you want to be positioned above these competitors for example, *store design* or atmospherics will need to be more attractive, so investing in flooring, shop fittings, décor, lighting and fixtures will enhance your positioning. If you choose to reposition above your department store competitor, your *customer service* will need to be superior so invest in customer service training for your staff to ensure the overall experience in your store is better and more consistent. Scrutinising your brand positioning in this way may highlight a major point-of-difference that your competitors are all online and you are not, for example.

Another example of repositioning the elements of the retail mix *is pricing*. Prices can be higher if you are positioned higher but not uncompetitive. Understand that consumers will pay more for the same thing but understand how much more. For example, if your direct competitor sells a well-known brand of food processor for $95 in their catalogue, you can get away with selling the same or very similar item for $99 but can you sell it for RRP$139 or above?

The answer lies with whether the market will bear the price difference. In this example, you risk sending a message to your customers that you are overpriced on your most recognised product brand and so everything in your store must be overpriced, even though it may not be. That is probably not the message you want to inadvertently send to your customers.

In 2011, 48% of shoppers used their smart phones to price check and 75% used mobile devices as part of their buying process including pricing research.[54] Some consumers will even go to the trouble of showing you that you are uncompetitive in-store via a smart phone! Imagine! *Ouch!*

Inflating the price or even selling at recommended retail price on a price sensitive item that can be easily found online or in a catalogue (or in a catalogue on-line) is short term and suicidal in today's Internet driven information age. If you sell that food processor for $139 to what I call a 'wood duck' customer, they *will* eventually find out you were not competitive and feel you *ripped them off*, even though you were only trying to make a reasonable margin!

They will tell 20 friends by word-of-mouth and who knows how many FB users who average 130 friends[55] each, all waiting to hear about how evil your retail brand is! They will rarely return to the store for a second time to get ripped off [in their mind] once again. Retailers generally cannot afford to be damaged by social media campaigns telling the global village about uncompetitive pricing.

Here is a quick table that is a short version of how to reposition your retail brand. The table is a simplified version of the 3-step brand positioning procedure[56] developed by Australian, Professor John Rossiter from the commerce faculty of the University of Wollongong, New South Wales. By answering the questions in the table you will be able to better formulate your plan to reposition and feel confident you have used sound marketing principles to do so.

3-step brand positioning

Step 1	TARGET-Who are your **target** customers?	CATEGORY-What **category** are you in and what customer need are you satisfying? Category: Need:	BENEFIT-What key **benefits** do you provide? 1. 2. 3. 4.
Step 2	DELIVERY-How will you believably **deliver** your brand promise?	UNIQUE- What are your **unique** points-of-difference?	1. 2. 3. 4.
Step 3	ATTRIBUTE- What is your key **attribute?**	BENEFIT-How will you tell the **benefits** of your brand to your customers?	EMOTION-How will you make an **emotional** connection to your customers through repositioning?

Quick Tips to step 2 reposition

1. **Decide** who you are and what you stand for
2. **Outline** your core values and align them with your brand personality
3. **Know** who your customers are
4. **Conduct** a simple analysis of where you are positioned with regard to your competitors
5. **Choose** your positioning i.e. higher, lower or line-ball in order to consolidate your retail strategy and capitalise on opportunities
6. **Incorporate** uniqueness in your repositioning
7. **Remember** to incorporate innovations and sustainability elements where possible
8. **Assess** your competitiveness on a global scale, not just locally
9. **Fill-in** the answers to the quick brand positioning table

3-rename

Many people get rebranding confused with renaming. Griffith University academic, Dr. Dale Miller cautions that a full rebrand may not necessarily incorporate a name change and that merely renaming your retail brand is not considered a rebrand.

Renaming is defined as changing your name in order to signal a shift in strategy or reposition to your customers, suppliers and staff (stakeholders).[57] Rebranding aims to differentiate brand positioning in the minds of all stakeholders and to create a distinctive identity from your competitors. Your brand name should define your identity and image and is the basis for awareness and communications.[58] A strong brand name is a valuable asset that adds to overall brand equity.[59]

The decision to rename may work against you through the loss of brand equity or recognition factor or it could act as a new beginning for your brand to move forward. Consider whether to rename or not very carefully as it is an important decision in the rebranding process.

To rename

The argument for renaming is that 'Small businesses are better served by rebranding their name and image in a short timeframe especially when existing brand notoriety is low. The powerful first impression on new customer segments made possible by professional brand redesign often outweighs an outdated or poorly designed image's weak brand recognition to existing customers'.[60]

If you agree with this statement, a name change may be the way to go. If you decide to dump your old brand name because you inherited it through an acquisition (purchase) or it has negative equity (reputation damage), there are a number of different ways to rename your brand. For example, a *descriptive brand* name will allow you to communicate more easily with your target markets.[61] Consider this story:

Butcher's personal service

An independent butcher was not trading well and his business had the previous owners brand attached to it. The previous owner operated several other stores in the area and the brand's customer service was known to be substandard. After discussing this in context, we agreed that it impacted negatively on the brand. Also, being associated with a brand that is not yours is out of your control and can lead to uncontrollable damage. We decided to drop the old name and rename as 'Stevo's Wholesale Meats'. Adding the word 'wholesale' to the name told the customer clearly that the prices are lower than major surrounding competitors and communicates the brand's positioning. Using the owner's name added a personal service message that his competitors cannot provide. *We all know the attractiveness of an independent butcher is the personal touch they provide!* **A rename can be entirely appropriate if your brand has a negative equity association**

Associative or *suggestive* names convey value association to your brand offer.[62] For example, Midas [shoes] associates with the 'midas touch' or turning everything into gold, suggesting a positive brand association to the name.

Abstract or *invented* names are useful for International brand names and trademark brands but may not convey brand meaning clearly.[63] The use of a person's name such as David Jones, Napoleon Perdis or Peter Alexander is known as patronymic naming. Retail giant IKEA has an *acronymic* name that stands for Ingvar Kamprad the founder, and Elmtaryd Agunnaryd, the town where he grew up.

When deciding on a new name, it's helpful to make an assessment of how much positive brand equity your current brand name owns. That is, think about how many people are aware of and recognise your brand and associate it with a positive experience. Consider if it is important to hold onto the *historical value* or *brand heritage* that your brand may possess. You may find the historical value is of utmost importance *or* you may find there is simply no benefit or even damage (negative brand equity) in retaining your old brand, even if it is fifty years old!

Your retail brand may have become irrelevant and consequently has no meaning to your target audience, in which case a rename can be entirely appropriate. Remember to ask yourself who your customers are now and into the future and what does your brand mean to *them.*

A patronymic brand that is your name, for example, may not hold any meaning to your customers or to your new target customers in today's contemporary context. It's like asking someone under fifteen if they know who Elvis is. For many, it has no meaning, is irrelevant or outdated. *Apologies to Elvis fans!* Consider this example:

'Sunbird'

Lee, a small independent food retailer in a very busy city mall has enjoyed some years of profit before the downturn but now his sales are slow, even though foot traffic in the food court where he is located, is excellent. There are a number of problems with Lee's model but most predominantly, his brand has no meaning to his customers and he has not updated his branding for some 8 years. Lee's brand 'Sunbird' which is his trading name and a rough translation of his family name in his first language, does not describe the food he serves or link to any meaning for his customers. Lee's product offer is sushi and hot noodle soup. Renaming the outlet 'Sushi & Soup' or 'Sunbird Sushi and Soup' would communicate to the hungry consumer what differentiates this business from other food retailers around it. Lee's former brand lacks *relevance* to his passing trade and part of the remedy is a full or partial rename. **Get in touch with your customers and send a strong relevant message about who you are and what you do**

Not to rename

You may come to the conclusion that you do not want or need to change your brand name. Abandoning an already established name is not always recommended because of the retained positive equity it may already posses. If you are satisfied that you have an effective retail brand and you are going to retain but refresh it, then building a bridge through incremental or gradual change from the old brand to the new, is a vital step to rebranding.[64]

If you wish to update your brand, logo, colour or font, it is important that you keep some of the core elements and personality of your current brand in the process.[65] That means retaining some of your core or peripheral features, especially if you have uniqueness or distinctiveness already on your side. Keeping those features is a great platform to work from and will help you develop your new revised brand identity.

Choose what you want to keep and choose what you want to update. The aim is to maintain brand notoriety or equity with your existing customer base whilst meeting the needs of additional market segments or new customers in order to capture growth. Remember that 'maintaining a connection between the old brand and the new brand can be vital in the rebranding process.' [66]

Can you think of a time when you were looking for your favourite product brand in the supermarket only to be confused by a new label or packaging that you didn't recognise? You probably experienced an initial 'disconnect' or uncertainty until you became used to the changes and felt more confident with purchasing the product in its new form. If the changes were substantial it may have created doubt about the brand and you may have walked away without buying it. If the changes were minor or incremental and it was pleasing but small, you simply accepted it and assumed that your favourite brand was updating with the times. Sound familiar?

In essence, if you have equity in your retail brand, the bigger the change, the bigger the disconnect risk you create so if you don't need to rename, incremental or gradual change is the best way to go.[67]

Corporate product brand label blunder

Some years ago, a large food manufacturer brand changed their canned veggie label. Angela, the newly appointed Head of Marketing, decided to change all the labels to a white background and update the pictures to make them smaller and more 'stylish' to appeal to a new customer segment. I was present for the concept delivery presentation. When the newly labeled stock arrived on the shelves, it was an immediate disaster. In the first week, sales dropped through the floor in all the major grocery chains and it was obvious to senior management that the label changes were to blame. The product was recalled and the old label reinstalled on supermarket shelves as quickly as possible. Sales returned to normal levels over the next few months and it was described as a very expensive mistake that cost millions! Today's label is similar to the original and hasn't changed *radically*, only incrementally, since that very costly mistake. **If you do not rename, incremental changes are most effective**

Refreshing your brand can be a way to regain contemporary relevance.[68] Corporate brands such as the Commonwealth Bank successfully moved to the shorter Commbank logo and contemporised the diamond logo artwork. In 1995, retail and product brand Nike, removed the brand name leaving the 'swoosh' as the updated logo. It soon became the world's most recognised symbol. Adidas shows its logo refreshed as black and white stripes in a landscape rectangle or triangle, a slight update from the clover shape of the past.

St. Vincent de Paul opportunity shops revised their brand name and logo to 'Vinnies' in order to breathe life into the brand and regain relevance with a younger audience. Fast food brand KFC updated its Colonial Saunders portrait art and font but retained the signature red and white to ensure the brand didn't lose equity as a result of the update. There is no doubt to customers that KFC is a contemporary and up-to-date brand that has retained its historic value and meaning.

Woolworths is an interesting Australian case of how a corporate retailer has revised its logo to reflect a more contemporary direction for the brand. The new green apple and outstretched arms logo (look closely) created by Hans Hulsbosch and launched in 2009, reflects the company's move toward environmental sustainability practices and statements of social corporate responsibility by using ethical and local suppliers and reducing their carbon footprint.

The new logo helped pave the way for store design upgrades and aligns with the company's strategic move toward a greener retailing story. I wonder if the folks at Woolies are planning to drop the name altogether using just the green apple as a recognisable symbol that shouts the Woolworths experience to their customers?

In summary, if you are not changing your name altogether, small changes that consumers can accept as legitimate revisions to your brand are the best way to go. 'Key sources of brand equity or worth should be preserved and amplified where appropriate'.[69]

Secret 12-Join forces

Combining your business with a competitor can be a way to gain market share, competitiveness and growth and represents a good reason to reposition and rename. Signing up with a larger organisation such as a buying group or franchise can help your business develop long term sustainability by buying better, diversifying your product brand portfolio and updating to best practices through better resourcing. It can also be a great way to prepare your business for sale.

Bob Beaumont of Beaumont Tiles suggests that in Australia, joining a franchise can strengthen specialty retail bringing more control over supply chain efficiencies, trading terms and buying power. Central distribution allows for bigger margins and less stock holding in retail outlets and national branding of stores and systems allows a saleable exit strategy for franchisees.[70]

Joining a group or franchise can be a very successful way of buying a growth or saleable exit strategy through improved resources, products, advertising and marketing and magnifies positive brand equity through adding to distribution points for already established retail brands.

Ace Hardware in the United States is an example of a chain of independently owned Californian stores that survived the 'bigbox' onslaught of the 90s due to stores joining forces, updating their RBM and combining their resources.

If you join a group or franchise it's important that you rename your business to suit that groups' existing brand in order for you to gain advantage from the brand's positioning, heritage and brand memory value it holds. In the big picture of marketing and advertising, it is likely that the new brand has greater equity than your previous brand. Remember, you are sending a clear message to your customers about who you are and what you do. That means dropping your old brand altogether and embracing the new.

What is your brand anyway?

Whilst visiting a store belonging to a buying group, I noticed the outside of the store was red and black. I asked Justin why the outside of his store was red when the group colour was yellow and black. He replied 'I hate yellow so I used red instead'. My next question was 'Why does your store have two names?' Justin replied 'What do you mean two names?' I said 'I mean you have your national name 'The Renovation Room' but you have added *Justin's* Renovation Room to it. Why?' He said 'I want to keep my name too.' This is a commonly taken approach by individually owned stores belonging to a buying group. However, it diminishes the equity in the 'Renovation Room' brand and confuses your brand message to your customers. **If you join a group or franchise, it's best to build more equity in the national retail brand name and let go of your old name**

Secret 13-Build brand strength

The two steps to reposition and rename (or not) your retail brand provide opportunities to improve your overall **brand strength** against your competitors. Brand strength is about who you are (brand identity), what you are (brand meaning), what your customers think or feel about you (brand responses) and what kind of connection they would like to have with you (brand relationships).[71]

Interbrand is the world's largest brand consultancy and publishers of the annual list of 'world's best retail brands'. Here is an easy checklist that I have adapted from Interbrand's 10 principles of brand strength.[72] Answer 'Yes' or 'No' to the questions below to check if you are on track with your repositioning and renaming plans to build your new brand strength.

Brand strength checklist

1. Created core brand values and understood target customers to build brand **clarity?**	Y / N
2. Applied time, influence and investment to build brand **commitment?**	Y / N
3. Protected legal, design and geographic dimensions to build brand **protection?**	Y / N
4. Adapted to market changes, challenges and opportunities to build brand **responsiveness?**	Y / N
5. Delivered heritage and core values to the customer to build brand **authenticity?**	Y / N
6. Fitted customer needs across demographics and geographies to build brand **relevance?**	Y / N
7. Positioned distinctively against competitors to build brand **differentiation?**	Y / N
8. Ensured that interaction points or 'touchpoints' with the brand are consistent to build brand **consistency?**	Y / N

9.	Created positive feelings and discussions through traditional and social media to build brand **presence?**	Y / N
10.	Achieved customer recognition and understanding of the brands distinctive qualities to build brand **understanding?**	Y / N

If you haven't answered 'Yes' to all these questions, *don't worry!* As you read the next section, all will become clearer as I outline how to redesign your retail brand. For now, think about the strategic processes involved in repositioning and the advantages or disadvantages to your brand of renaming.

Not everything you read in the next section will apply to your business, but certainly there will be opportunities to lengthen your to-do list, so be sure to jot them down as you read. Redesigning is the biggest and most expensive step in the rebranding process and involves change through action.

I hope you enjoy the journey in the pages ahead and that this step helps you breathe fresh, vibrant and exciting ideas into your new innovative and sustainable RBM and retail brand. *Fantastic!*

Quick Tips to step 3 rename

1. **Remember** that renaming alone is not rebranding
2. **Consider** a descriptive name if you rename
3. **Rename** if you join a group or franchise
4. **Think** about new customer segments if you are renaming
5. **Build** a bridge between the old brand and the new brand if you are not renaming, just updating
6. **Check** if you have carried out the 10 principles to brand strength

4-redesign

The re-tail mix

Your retail mix is made up of the elements of location, layout, store design, merchandise assortment, visual merchandising, pricing, promotions and customer service.[73] Today's consumer demands an overall higher standard of retailing that not only incorporates a unique in-store experience through all of these mix elements, but presumes online accessibility to your retail brand through websites and social media. This is why I call it the *re-tail* mix as opposed to the traditional *retail* mix. Can you think of a market leading brand that cannot be found on Google, does not have a website or does not engage with consumers via social media platforms?

This section outlines how to redesign the elements of the traditional in-store retail mix and covers the essential online elements for a contemporary and diversified approach to your re-tail business model. All of these distinctive elements require careful consideration in order to align with your brand's core values, personality and image and incorporate sustainability and innovation simultaneously.

Remember, it's your uniqueness and how you communicate it that will set you apart and help you gain your important competitive advantage. So, be bold and brave and reinvent your re-tail mix to make a statement that makes you stand out from the crowd and tells your customers clearly *who you are and what you do.*

Secret 14-Choose the right location

Your store location should aid in generating foot traffic, contribute to the convenience of the shopper, enhance the customer's overall shopping experience and strengthen your retail brand's image.[74]

Without the best possible location, traffic numbers may be suffering and you could be losing customers without even knowing it. For example, I have experienced many retail stores that have a great re-tail mix combination but have inadequate parking at their store location, so it's impossible to get a parking space. If you are a destination store, particularly in a primary business street (high street) location, your customers must be able to park otherwise you risk them driving away to a competitor who *does* have adequate parking.

If your potential customers don't enter your store to start with because they have not been able to secure a suitable parking space, they cannot enjoy your brand's in-store experience and more importantly, you cannot measure that foot traffic loss. I have seen many specialty retailers with three or four parking spaces at their store and the staff park in those spaces all day, *every day*! Some store personnel actually put their names on the parking bays! I suggest that these parking spaces are priceless to your business and so should be kept available in order to contribute to the overall convenience of your customers.

Ask yourself if your retail brand will be best served in a shopping mall or in a high street location. Be aware of where the central hub in your retail precinct is located. Take note if it has moved to a different area in recent years because of a new development. Perhaps the post office moved, taking with it your passing trade.

It is common to find small retailers situated in areas with falling traffic numbers due to new buildings or developments that have relocated main shopping precincts away from original shopping hubs. The rent hasn't gone down but the traffic numbers have!

Do you know if foot traffic numbers to your store are increasing or decreasing? This type of information can be used to ascertain if your location is still serving you well. Shopping centre marketing managers can tell you exactly how many people have entered your centre on a yearly or monthly basis and this is a good way to gauge what is happening around you.

High street locations can be equipped with low cost devices that measure traffic numbers through counting how many wireless devices have passed by or into your store.[75] You can embark on a head count project to determine how many customers are entering your store daily and weekly to measure traffic numbers over time and help determine if a move may be necessary to improve your customer volume.

You may not be able to immediately improve your store location but a situation analysis will help you focus on planning future expansions or consolidations. If you decide a move is in order, consider new locations that may better align with your revised core brand values like sustainable 'green' buildings or renovated extensions to shopping malls. Perhaps a high street location may be a good option for you to help decrease your carbon footprint and improve energy efficiencies to reinforce your overall brand positioning.

Your economic and environmental sustainability can be improved by building your own retail site where you are able to rent back to yourself and take control of energy usage and other innovations that save you money and enhance your RBM.

If you are planning to open your first store, a shopping centre casual mall lease or kiosk may be just the thing to improve the online profile of your budding new brand. Consider if your retail brand is right for the mall and if the mall is right for your retail brand before making a commitment to a medium to long-term lease.

Mall location

A move into a mall or shopping centre may help you by increasing passing traffic numbers due to surrounding 'anchor' retailers that draw the numbers for you. Below are some considerations to ponder if you are to make the right location decision to enhance your retail brand.

1. Woolworths, Target, Kmart, Myer, David Jones, Aldi, Lowes and other large retailers are all considered anchor stores that are shopping destinations and will enhance your exposure to passing foot traffic due to their proximity to your store.
2. Competitive and complimentary shop clusters can enhance your foot traffic so locating your store close to your competitors gives customers more reasons to pass by. If you are a boutique fashion retailer, for example, make sure you are positioned near other fashion outlets within the mall. Customers like choice when shopping and the more stores that are grouped together, the greater the destination and variety. Higher foot traffic numbers therefore pass the location.

3. Negotiate the best possible position with your centre or leasing manager and always be on the lookout for better locations as other leases are renewed or become available.
4. Be aware of leasing terms and conditions and always read the fine print.
5. Match your brand to the mall's customers or demographic.

Mall location

Advantages	Disadvantages
High foot traffic numbers	Higher rent
Impulse shoppers	Less flexible rent negotiations
Ample parking	Further for customers to walk
Free shopping centre marketing	Smaller store
Assistance from centre staff	Limited storage
Manageable shop size	Pay % of profits to centre (in some
Less costly to shop fit smaller space	cases)
High security	Possible restrictions on mixed
	revenue income streams
	Signage restrictions
	Loading and access difficulties
	Compulsory shop refits
	Fixed trading hours
	Small windows

High street location

As we see a trend toward community based shopping, growers markets and local supply, a high street location can help to identify you as a unique destination store. Your brand personality and core values can shine through effective signage and an engaging shop front. Consider these points:

1. Positioning yourself close to cafés and hubs will ensure higher foot traffic to your store.
2. Competitive and complimentary shop clusters will help increase foot traffic.
3. Negotiating your rent conditions when vacancy rates are high puts you in the drivers seat and gives you choice.
4. Consider that ample parking adds to convenience for your shoppers and is vitally important.

High Street location

Advantages	Disadvantages
More unique destination branding opportunity	Less passing foot traffic
Larger space	Limited parking
Lower rent per square metre	Higher cost to shop fit larger store
More flexible rent negotiations	Higher overhead costs as larger space
Often can have better signage	Council restrictions may apply to signage
Use of larger windows	Low security
Can stock larger merchandise assortment	
More lease flexibility	
More flexible or longer trading hours	
Sub letting opportunities	
Convenience of access	
Warehousing/storage for e-tail business	

Signage, car parking, road signs, driveways and entry points, traffic lights, roundabouts, u–turns and loading areas are all access factors that impact the experience of arriving and departing from your store. It's a good idea to conduct an audit for what it's like for a new customer to find you in your high street or mall location. For example, are you easy to see? Is your signage faded or is a tree blocking your visibility?

Many consumers now look for information about your location via their smart phones. Does anyone really use the yellow or white pages anymore? Pretend that you are a potential new customer and Google your store to see what comes up in your search. If there is a problem finding your business online because of an old address, phone, name or logo, there will most definitely be a problem finding you in real life!

Customers who can't find you easily and abort their search never come into your store and tell you they gave up do they? It's important to fix any incorrect details to ensure your **location** is easy to find and easy to access.

Quick Tips to choose the right location

1. **Check** that your location generates foot traffic, contributes to the convenience of the shopper, enhances the customer's overall shopping experience and strengthens your retail brand's image
2. **Conduct** an analysis of your store's location and foot traffic
3. **Decide** which location aligns best with your retail brand strategy
4. **Draw up** an action plan for your location change if applicable
5. **Ensure** that there is adequate parking for your customers
6. **Google** your digital search information to make sure it is correct and you are easy to find and easy to access

Secret 15-Maximise your layout

You are paying the same overhead rental cost per square metre at the back of the store as you are at the front, so it is important that you achieve the highest possible sales return throughout the entire store. The optimal floor layout will maximise selling opportunities and sales conversions at no additional cost to your business through effective fixture, category and product placement. Market leaders measure their store layout performance in terms of dollar return per square centimetre. Let's start with your overall store **layout** and work down to the centimetres.

Destination control

Within the context of interior floor layouts, the term 'destination' means a fixture, category or product that customers walk to no matter where you position it. The most obvious and powerful destination fixture is your counter. A very high percentage of your customers walk to your counter for service and transactions and so it can be used to manipulate traffic flow to the rear.

Placing your counter at the rear allows you to control unaware customers to walk through the greater area of your store on the way to the destination fixture, your counter. Shoppers are also more likely to stay longer when they are further in your store and shoppers that stay longer, buy more.

Whilst your counter is an important fixture and you may need it to process sales, reducing it to the smallest workable size will enhance selling opportunities by increasing floor space for more merchandise. Oversized counters can act as a barrier to interactions between customers and staff and inhibit customer service standards by providing a place for staff to congregate. They can often collect unsightly mess and personal belongings that project an unprofessional first impression.

The Apple store model has eliminated the need for service counters altogether by equipping staff with iPod touch card readers for fast transactions anywhere in the store. Further to that, the brand now encourages consumers to self-transact in-store using personal iPhones to complete purchases.

This eliminates the need for costly personal selling to those customers who do not require it and average customer transaction times are minimised. Modern consumers scan items for payment and happily provide email addresses during transactions in order to get receipts via their smart phones. This information is then used at a later date for marketing communications. *Brilliant!*

Eliminating the need for a service and transaction counter is certainly innovative and maximises volume of sales whilst minimising customer wait times. It also abolishes the dreaded queue and the need for checkouts that often come with high volume retail models. The additional floor space gained by eliminating service counters allows more room around fixtures adding to the spacious store design that aligns with the brand's contemporary positioning. The Apple 'Genius Bar' provides an experiential destination fixture where product demonstrations and tutorial appointments are conducted. *You guessed it! It's located at the rear!*

Let's say that your counter is at the front of your store. Watch carefully as your customers walk to it and ignore other parts of your floor. Counter placement at the front actually creates low traffic areas for a large proportion of your layout where few customers browse. These areas are known as 'cold spots' that inhibit sales returns from those areas due to little attention from shoppers.

Hotspot control

Cold spots do not provide an acceptable dollar return per square metre. Hot spots, on the other hand, have the most exposure to consumers, turn over the highest volume of stock and are highly desirable profit centres that are your most valuable store real estate. Warm spots are peripheral areas surrounding hotspots that sell more than cold spots but significantly less than hotspots. You have probably heard about what I call **hotspot control** before, but are you capitalising on this concept by using these strategies in your store layout right now?

It makes perfect sense to maximise hotspots and minimise coldspots when redesigning small store layouts, and many market leaders also use this strategy. An example is IKEA, who direct traffic flow within their store to maximise sales, effectively eliminating cold spots altogether.

If you happen to fall in the small demographic of the population who refuse to go to IKEA because you don't like to be told where to walk, the retail giant understands that their brand cannot appeal to every single demographic or personality type. IKEA are happy to report however, that their worldwide market share increased by 9.5% in 2012 totalling AUD\$40.7bn and that 690 million store visitors clicked on their website one billion times![76] *Wow!*

Your immediate reaction about moving your counter may be that your counter at the front serves as security against theft or what market leaders call 'shrinkage'. I hear you loud and clear. Nobody feels good about losing money through theft, but consider this: A leading liquor chain store loses $90,000 per month due to shrinkage. The organisation and its managers understand that if they do not incorporate hotspot floor stacks at the front, the *opportunity cost* is far greater. The $90,000 shrinkage represents less than 9% of monthly turnover but negative impacts on turnover due to the absence of primary hotspots at the front can be measured as far greater.

So, if a specialty retailer loses $100 a month in shrinkage due to counter positioning at the rear, it's best to consider that shrinkage as a cost of doing business (COB) and a trade-off for higher overall sales from the front of the store.

Hundreds of my retail clients have gone through the pain of moving counters and fixtures in order to improve traffic flows and gain control of primary selling hotspots at the front of their stores. Without exception, this strategy works well to return immediate sales growth. Eliminate cold spots in small stores by placing counters and destination brands, categories or products at the rear to guarantee traffic flow to those areas.

Are you thinking about what your destination category or product brand might be by now? Market leaders use destination categories, product brands and even individual products to create hotspots around their stores and what's more, they multiply hotspot merchandising control on three levels for maximum impact!

Primary hotspots include entrance areas, end caps (gondola ends), counters and destination categories or products. Secondary hotspots include display positioning within categories such as merchandising bins and floor stacks and tertiary hotspots are eye level positioning on fixtures within every category around the store.

Similar to the IKEA model, supermarket layouts plan traffic flow within the store and position products on gondola ends (primary hotspots) to maximise customer exposure to those products. Gondola end positioning in the past, has been proven to increase sales by up to 229%![77] In addition, the placement of milk (a destination product) at the back of the store ensures traffic flows to the rear, further eliminating cold spots.

Some market leading retailers charge manufacturer brands a fee for premium hotspot positioning within their stores. Suppliers gain maximum return on their promotional investments (product discounts and advertising) through hotspot product exposure and retailers gain incremental revenue (money for placement) through effective and efficient *paid placement displays.*

An example of **hotspot control** is let's say you have a clothing store and you stock a well-known brand of fashion that is exclusive to you in your geographic area. You believe the brand pulls customers into your store. The products are highly priced but margin is skinny in order to compete with online sellers. The brand has its own retail outlets that have incorporated the vertical supply model, which is further impacting on your diminishing margins. This brand appears on the outside of your shop front and in your window displays.

Let me ask you, does it make economic sense to merchandise this brand at the front of your store if it can be used effectively to eliminate a cold spot at the rear and open up spaces for higher margin brands or paid placement displays at the front that earn you more money? Placing your destination category or brand as far into the store as possible without negatively impacting upon sales is what successful market leaders do.

For example, large sporting stores place the shoe category on the rear wall to entice shoppers to the back of their stores. Nespresso place the free coffee tasting bar to the rear to ensure customer traffic flows to the back of the store. Destination categories and products should have effective signage and excellent lighting to highlight these areas and ensure they are turned into hotspots.

Over the last two decades I have observed and measured sales growth ranging anywhere from 10% to an incredible 200%! The improvement is the result of incorporating these layout strategies and focusing on building, maintaining and controlling hotspot merchandising in primary, secondary and tertiary positions throughout the entire store. Experimenting with these principles is the best way to find out what works best in your store environment. *It's incredibly powerful stuff!*

Once your counter and destination category or product is well positioned, the rest of your store layout can now be planned taking **hotspot control** into account. In a small store environment, the path from the front door to the counter is called your 'promotional corridor'. It represents a hotspot pathway for strategic product placement that allows merchandise to be highly exposed. It is absolutely the area that returns the highest volume or highest margin of sales, or in a perfect retail world, *both!*

Reinvented computers

> TC, the marketing manager of a neighbourhood shopping mall wanted to help an independent computer store that was not trading well. The retailer was in a prime location at an entry point to the centre but sales were poor. After two full days of hands-on reinvention of the windows, categories, hotspots, pricing and ticketing standards the store was overhauled using all the layout and visual merchandising principles outlined in this section. TC reported that in the 6 weeks following the reinvention, sales increased by 200%! I know it's hard to believe, but it's absolutely true. **This stuff really, really works! Just ask TC!**

Margin control

Selling high volumes of high margin merchandise is undoubtedly a key strategy that helps maintain economic sustainability. I call this tactic **margin control.** Have you ever pondered why the first category you see in department stores is cosmetics or why Target and Kmart have clothing at the front? Highest percentage of *profit margin* is the answer.

American, Harry Selfridge was arguably the first retailer to place the highly profitable perfume counter in the best position on the ground floor of his hugely successful turn of the century department store. He was also said to be the innovator who introduced experiential retailing strategies such as taking products out from behind glass so customers could try the merchandise. Selfridge's perfume counter was the most profitable store category and so it was placed to maximise volume of highest margin at the front of the store.

This tactic is widely considered today as best practice in layout strategy. You can implement it in your store right now by placing products or categories with the highest margin in the best hotspot positions.

How does margin control theory impact the placement of racks and dump bins of markdowns with little or no margin? Essentially, placing these displays at the front of your store will sell high volumes of no profit. Some specialty retailers believe it's a way to get customers to stop. Yes, it can stop customers momentarily, but for all the wrong reasons. You want customers to stop and come into your store for your unique shopping experience at sustainable healthy margin, not to buy a $10 markdown with zero profit margin attached. I'm sure you will agree that there is an opportunity cost attached to placing low margin lines in hotspot locations, especially for long periods of time.

Market leaders, especially fashion retailers, position sale racks and markdowns at the rear so customers must walk past full margin lines to get to the bargains. Many fashion retailers now call these racks the 'last of the best sellers'. Here's a summary of hotspot and margin control principles to incorporate into your store that will improve your profitability:

Hotspot and margin control

Hot Spots	Entrance and payment areas Gondola ends/categories Eye level	High turnover + high margin	=Highly desirable
Warm spots	Peripheral traffic areas Above and below eye level	Medium turnover	=Less desirable
Cold spots	Low customer traffic areas Far corners, low shelf/high shelf	Low or no turnover	=Not desirable

Interestingly, shoppers in Australia, New Zealand, Japan, India and the UK naturally look and walk to the left when entering stores, standing on escalators and walking down footpaths. The reverse is true in the Americas, China, Europe and Scandinavia where the population drive cars on the right hand side of the road. This rule is cleverly termed the 'Cars Rule the World' (CRTW) law of retail traffic[78] and is consumer behaviour that should be considered when planning for the best possible retail floor layouts.

The crucial time to consider incorporating these layout principles is during the store design and set-up phases. If you are unsure about how to plan or re-plan your store layout, this diagram with hotspots highlighted in black, shows how effective counter positioning pushes customer traffic to the rear and around the entire fashion outlet. This strategy creates a promotional corridor with hotspot displays en route to the fixture destination that is your counter and the sale rack area and is a model that can be applied to any retail segment.

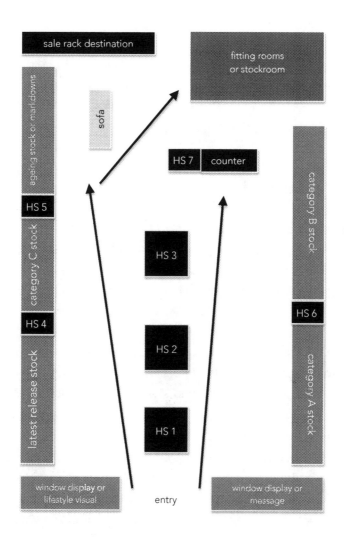

Hotspot 1= new product with high margin

Hotspot 2= latest product

Hotspot 3= latest product

Hotspot 4=category C stock hotspot display

Hotspot 5=category C hotspot display

Hotspot 6=category A hotspot display

Hotspot 7= impulse lines

Don't move that!

> When retailers say, 'Don't move that. It sells really well where it is at the front!' I say, 'No matter what you put there, it will sell because it's a hot spot. I hope it's got good margin!' **Place high margin merchandise in hotspots**

Fast and efficient sales

Consider that enabling **fast and efficient sales** to occur is a minimum service standard that all contemporary consumers have come to expect as a convenience from today's retailers. It plays an essential role in the buying habits of consumers and thus the layout planning of your store.

Without a doubt, every customer deserves great service and a positive experience in your store. Strategies can be incorporated into category management and shelf management that enable customers to produce fast and efficient sales (self-serve) when they want to (just browsing) or when they need to (no available staff). This still allows you to offer the best possible personalised service to those customers who want it or those customers who need it, whilst remaining customers are enabled to help themselves just like the remarkably successful Apple retail store model.

A single staff member can serve exactly *one* customer at a time in order to deliver excellent service, so what happens to every single customer when you have five at once and only four staff serving? Today's customers do not want to wait especially if they only need to ask a question like where is product X or how much is product Y. Customers in country areas tend to wait a little longer for personalised service than their city counterparts, but nobody wants to wait if all they need to do is pick up a refill or make a simple selection, pay, and go.

In Australia, wages and overheads are higher than in any other part of the world so it is essential to maximise sales volumes at the lowest possible cost to the business (minimal staff). Customers must be able to at least begin their buying process without necessarily interacting with staff. Forcing customers to wait by not incorporating a self-serve element into your model is *not* a hallmark of excellent service and does not align with a sustainable RBM that demands higher sales volumes at lower costs. Enabling faster and more efficient sales through self-serve is economically sustainable and takes pressure off unaffordable personalised selling costs.

I believe that giving *every single customer* personalised service is no longer viable in terms of costs, especially for smaller retailers. Can you imagine if your market leading competitors employed enough staff to serve every single customer at once? Yet it is often an expectation of small retailers to do just that.

Enabling fast and efficient sales is a weapon that specialty retailers can incorporate to increase turnover and lower overhead costs. It's a formula to enhance profitability that really works. Consider that a portion of your customers can and will self-serve, if you enable them. Consider that every self-serve customer is one that does not cost your business time and wages and consider that self-serving customers make up a growing percentage of your sustainable and more competitive RBM.

Think of fast and efficient sales in these ways:

- It is impossible to offer personalised service for every single customer if you are to have the volume of customers required to sustain your business.
- Effective category and shelf management encourages those customers who are happy to self-serve, to do so. It relieves pressure from staffing levels and increases volume of sales.
- Fast and efficient sales free up your time to deliver excellent service to those customers who do require your help and expertise.
- Some customer segments do not want personalised service straight away upon entering your store. They simply want to browse and be greeted by a friendly face until they are ready to engage with staff.
- Fast and efficient sales are a necessary innovation in your business to gain relevance and sustainability into the future.

The consumer buying process (CBP)

Laying out your store, categories and products according to how your customers shop, will allow faster and more efficient sales to take place. I call this enabling the **consumer buying process (CBP).** The CBP may vary slightly from person to person, however, the basic process outlines the emotional and cognitive (thought) steps that a consumer goes through when making selection and purchase choices.

Each category or product segment may differ so it's important to look at each product and match up the CBP with the layout of the category or brand to which it is being applied. If you layout your store, categories and products to enable the CBP, fast and efficient sales become a part of everyday sustainable business.

The risk of losing customers out the door because they have to wait to ask simple questions that good category and shelf management strategies can answer, diminishes greatly whilst sales volumes improve significantly. It's a formula to success.

'I can't find the diary I want'

David the Newsagent had a large table of diaries in the middle of his store and arranged them according to supplier for ease of reorder. Before deciding how to re-merchandise the table, I observed how passersby were browsing the stock. Customers were picking up a couple of diaries at a time, opening them, looking inside, putting them down and hurrying off. I asked myself, what the CBP is for a desk diary. As a customer, my first consideration is size. Therefore, all A4, A5 and smaller sizes are arranged together. Days-to-a-page is the second consideration so diaries are then arranged in days to a page within their sizes. The next consideration in the buying process is colour, so colour blocking the fashion diaries in a section will enable the CBP further. Once the new layout was implemented, the diaries flew off the table. *Sold out!* David was happy! **Lay out merchandise according to how the shopper shops**

Recently, I saw a TV program that showed the next shift in grocery retailing as a trolley scanner where items scan automatically as you select them. Supermarkets are now looking at technology where the exit gates scan all the grocery items as you push the trolley through them. *Imagine!* The grocer simply charges your credit card for the amount and off you go. No queuing or self-serve checkouts only purely convenient shopping at the lowest cost to the retailer. This innovation takes self-service retailing to another level and can't help but make you think about the innovative possibilities technology will bring to the future. There's no stopping the self-serve trend. How will you compete? **Self-serve is the only sustainable way to manage customer and sales volume increases**

Category management

In my experience, some retailers define categories in-line with supplier recommendations, by what is easiest for reordering systems or because products simply 'fit' into an available space. This is not considered an effective category management plan.

There are a number of ways to manage categories that will enhance faster and more efficient sales, volume and profitability. It generally depends on your market segment and what best suits the product and CBP involved with the purchase. How you arrange your categories depends entirely on how your customers naturally shop.

One way to arrange merchandise is to think of your shop as a small department store with several *product* categories or sections. Market leaders aim to make shopping easier for customers and enable higher sales volumes through the use of *margin control.* They plan and execute every category position and product placement down to the inch or centimetre in order to gain and measure the best possible dollar return on retail space.

Positioning of categories within the store and positioning of products within the category must where possible, make sense to your customers, enable maximum exposure of high margin lines and enable fast and efficient sales.

Do your customers shop by brand, colour, size, style, price or a combination of factors? In supermarkets, customers shop by product category first, then price or brand. For example, let's say Irène wants canned beetroot for a salad. She finds the aisle or category sign that says 'canned vegetables' and walks to the canned veggie section to look for beetroot. She finds all brands, sizes and prices available together in one location. Irène chooses the brand she wants today, let's say it's Golden Circle 400g. She can switch from brand to price as her first consideration depending on her consumer buying process on that day.

Other factors impacting on her decision are positioning, labeling, promotions, advertising, value perception and so on. Irène finds her favourite brand on the shelf by recognising the familiar brand label and logo and then selects the size she wants. She notices it is on special, thinks to herself: 'Bonus, that seals the deal' or opts to pay full price for her preferred brand and goes to the [self-serve] checkout, pays and leaves. This is an example where store merchandising is designed to fit Irène's buying process and where Irène is perfectly enabled to serve herself.

Grocery retailers are particularly good at enabling fast and efficient sales based on category layouts that match the consumer buying process. An *ineffective* category layout in this example, would be merchandising by brand first. The grocer would place all of the Golden Circle products in one location across product categories and call it the 'Golden Circle aisle', creating a brand category as opposed to a product category.

The problem with this example is that Irène may not be able to remember the name of her favourite brand and she would not be exposed to other available brands in that section that may have a higher margin for the grocer.

Many specialty retailers do not lay out their stores according to how their customers shop and so the customer is unable to self-serve. The retailer is then tied to providing costly personalised service to every single customer on every single question or request. Often this approach creates frustrating waiting times for customers and in worst-case scenarios, customers that leave stores empty handed and go looking for environments where wait times are minimised and they can find what they need quickly and without assistance.

Department stores such as Myer, David Jones, Macy's, Harrods, Nordstrom, Neiman Marcus, Harvey Nichols and Selfridges/ Sears lay out much of their merchandise by category i.e. women's fashion or men's fashion and then by brand (Espirit, Fossil, Marcs, Tommy Hilfiger etc). This category management strategy is used by market leaders in many retail segments including paint and hardware, electronics, fashion, food, stationery and sporting goods and can most definitely be applied in specialty store retailing as a best practice standard.

Australian liquor giant, Dan Murphy, owned by Woolworths, formerly laid out wine in their stores according to region. *Very sophisticated indeed!* However, customers couldn't remember what region their favourite Chardonnay, Pinot or Shiraz came from and so endlessly wandered around the store looking for a vaguely familiar label until finally settling for something they thought was close. Since the retail giant re-merchandised by varietal, that is, arranged categories by wine type such as Chardonnay, Pinot and Shiraz, customers are able to find their favourite wines easily. Now that the products' merchandising strategy has been matched with the CBP fast and efficient sales volumes have increased! *Voilà!*

Another way to lay out categories is by colour. Stationery retailer 'Smiggle' lays out its stores by arranging products into colour groups. Customers shop for the products they want by looking in the colour section that appeals to them most. This is an effective way to get consumers to browse across product groups and encourages them to pick up more than one item at a time, increasing average sale dollars.

This successful specialty retailer actually orders its product manufacturing to suit the colours that will be featured in its merchandising strategy. This creates a very effective visual impact on passing consumers that is synonymous with the brand's contemporary, unique and fashionable appeal.

As I mentioned, each retail category and sub-category may require a slightly different approach when it comes to matching the merchandising with the CBP. Essentially, decisions for how products are to be laid out come down to the consumer's buying behaviour and enabling their buying process to occur at the lowest possible cost to the business. The easiest way to gain knowledge into the best practice standards that can be applied to your environment is to analyse examples of effective category management by market leaders in your segment.

In summary, effective category management is key to growing fast and efficient sales, which is a driver of economic sustainability. It is a minimum benchmark in today's customer service standards that allows and encourages consumers to navigate around the store at low cost to the business. These store layout principles lay the foundation to ensure sales are maximised and is a critical factor for careful consideration during the store design or redesign phase.

Maps sell by geographic category not product category

Chris, a specialty map seller with six outlets, wanted an assessment of merchandising standards to improve sales. I asked Chris, 'What are the key questions that your customers ask you?' Eventually, she confessed that many customers asked where to find products X, Y and Z. This indicated that Chris' stores were either not well signed or not well laid out or possibly, both. Customers commonly asked for products by geography. That is, they wanted maps, books, guides and so on, to do with the areas they were going to visit or study. This retailer placed all hiking maps together, all lonely planets together, all food guides together etc. making it incredibly difficult for customers to find what they wanted. There are next to zero fast and efficient sales with this product category management strategy. The best way for Chris to enable self-selection for her customers is to use the four walls as continents of the world and create categories that are laid out by geography and then alphabetical. This would allow customers to find what they want with ease and increase add-on sales of impulse items related to the first purchase. **Layout your store according to how your shopper shops for fast and efficient sales**

Quick Tips to maximise your layout

1. **Position** your counter and destination category, brand or product toward the rear
2. **Categorise** your products to enable the consumer buying process (CBP)
3. **Incorporate** hotspot control
4. **Place** high margin lines in hotspots and markdowns at the rear
5. **Enable** self-service as a priority
6. **Look** to market leaders for insight into best category management decisions

Secret 16-Sass-up your store design

Today's consumer expects a higher standard of store environment and total brand experience than ever before. Younger generations have expectations that far exceed those of Gen X and the baby boomer generation. Market leading retailers strive to deliver newer and higher standards that incorporate sustainability and innovation. Market leaders constantly evolve.

Store design amounts to a first impression and is another expression of who you are and what you do. Your store is an important interaction or 'touchpoint' with your brand. Signage and frontage, flooring, lighting, colours, finishes, fixtures, music and window displays can all add strength or detract from your brand story.

Marketing Professors Kusum Ailiwadi and Kevin Lane Keller at the Tuck school of Business in New Hampshire, USA state that:

'A pleasing in-store atmosphere encourages consumers to visit more often, stay longer and buy more. It improves consumers' perceptions of merchandise quality and consumers tend to associate it with higher prices. An appealing in-store atmosphere crafts a unique store image and establishes differentiation. Even if the products and brands stocked by a retailer are similar to others, the ability to create a strong in-store personality and rich experiences can play a crucial role in building retailer brand equity'.[79]

It's important to consider that pitching your store design and visual merchandising slightly above your brand positioning will enhance the customer's perception of value. Pitching your store design and visual merchandising below your brand positioning will create the negative perception of over pricing or asking too much for your goods. *Food for thought!*

Signage and frontage

Your store exterior projects everything you want to say and sometimes exactly what you don't want to say about your brand to your customers and competitors. It is the face of your brand. If your storefront is the only touchpoint your customers have with your brand, it is vitally important that you place a lot of focus on what the front of your store says to passersby. External signage should connect with your customer segments and again, clearly outline who you are and what you do. It must be relevant and up-to-date and align with your brand identity.

For example, do you really need to put your phone number on the store exterior or would it be better to put your web address? With the increase in consumers using mobile devices to find information, a web address may be more relevant than a phone number providing that the information is correct and up-to-date. You have two seconds to persuade a consumer to walk into your store using your frontage to entice them. *That's it! Can you do it?* Many stores lose their customers at this crucial first step in the buying process without even being aware of it.

Disused signage that remains visible on vacant buildings sends a negative message about your retail brand. If you move, its best to take down any remnants of your brand in order to avoid sending the message that you are no longer in business. Placing a message on the entry with your new address is a good idea to direct customers to your new location. I recently noticed that my local Blockbuster (video brand) has closed its doors. The brand signage still visible above the empty shop implies to consumers that the brand no longer exists. This further damages the struggling brand as it continues to rent DVD's from kiosks strategically placed in my area.

Your store frontage is where you can express your unique brand message and imprint your first impression on those new customer segments that are essential to capturing growth through rebranding. Be fearless and show your brand personality on your store frontage. Connect with your customers and your new target segments. Be sure to incorporate sustainable materials and messages, lighting, energy saving devices and innovation where possible. The passing consumer must first be enticed by your store exterior before the interior is ever experienced!

First impressions count

Recently, I ran a merchandising checklist over Lahood's Sydney paint store to highlight opportunities for improvement and areas to work on during my visit. The checklist started at the front of the store with the car park and garden. The car park was visibly littered and was not up to standard so I grabbed a garbage bag and began collecting rubbish. After collecting two full bags of garbage, I walked into the store, garbage bags in hand and showed Mr. Lahood what I had collected from the front of his store. He could not believe that every day he parked his Range Rover in that car park and did not see how bad it looked to new customers. He was devastated. **Checklists can be used to help gain objectivity and avoid 'retail blindness'**

Flooring

The reason I have put flooring and lighting next in line is because I believe they are the most important elements in store design for specialty retailers on a budget. The impact they make on first impressions far outweighs the impact made on customers by fixtures and wall colours.

Using natural and timber floor finishes, polished or whitewashed concrete conveys a contemporary message and is often less costly than carpet or tiles. Taking it back to basics where less is more will make your merchandise stand out in your store and help you gain attention from shoppers. Often, specialty retailers see the floor as the last thing on their list to improve. I put it right at the top of the list along with lighting!

Lighting

Lighting effects are essential to create environments that enhance the consumers overall brand and shopping experience. Together flooring and lighting are the two most powerful elements to create ambience or 'a vibe' for your brand. Many specialty retailers are concerned that dark colour schemes make stores look too small or dark. If your store is too dark, use more lighting to control the effect you want on your merchandise. Market leading retailers often block out daylight in order to better control lighting and regain valuable window space for wall fixtures.

Among many leading retail brands that invest heavily in lighting to create a unique in-store ambiance are American brands Abercrombie and Fitch and Ralph Lauren. These re-tailers have created distinctive shopping environments that augment the uniqueness of their brands. Re-tailers in Australia such as Universal Store, Dusk, the Body Shop and countless others use lighting to create powerful shopping environments that highlight their brand's points of difference by accentuating merchandise and creating shopping habitats for their in-store customers.

Varied lighting is the best way to light your store. Harsh fluorescent lights make everything look unattractive, especially in fitting rooms! If you sell fashion, go into Country Road or Abercrombie and Fitch and try something on. I swear the lighting in those fitting rooms makes every thing look thinner and *absolutely fabulous*!

Your fitting rooms should be free from boxes or unused fixtures and should make your customers feel like a million bucks, especially if you only have one. Fitting rooms are where fashion customers make their buying decisions and so need to be treated as important money making cubicles. Invest in lighting and décor to make sure your customers feel and look good when they are making important buying decisions *and put up extra hooks for handbags and shopping bags please!*

There are so many new and interesting lighting designs now available that are environmentally friendly *and* stylish. Here are some different lighting standards that you can use as a benchmark. Note that the general pattern system equipped in the majority of specialty retail sites is considered not adequate in today's competitive environment.

1. General Pattern System is **not adequate**
    It is a pattern of lights (usually fluorescent tubes) providing general lighting across the store. There is no regard to the location of the merchandise or fixtures.

This system is standard in most buildings but there will be a lack of emphasis on focal points and lighting will be at one level with no variance or control. This system will not allow your brand to stand out or make a statement and is generally mixed with high levels of daylight.

2. Specific System is a **minimum standard**
   It employs a layout of lights determined by the location of merchandise displays (fixtures, shelving, gondolas etc). It is tailored to emphasize the merchandise and defines merchandise areas from other areas.

3. Flexible System is **desirable**
   Employs a pattern of outlets of a temporary nature. You can move lights along tracks or move the lighting around the store where appropriate. This system allows you to regularly change displays around the store.

4. Supplementary lighting is **most desirable**
   Lighting on vertical wall displays (shelving) is important because of the favorable viewing angle, the impact on the visual environment and because wall displays are prime profit centres. Complete control over lighting is best with dimmers or separate switches to change lighting effects easily. Consumers must be able to clearly read labeling under lights and merchandise and hotspots can be highlighted with this standard.

Lighting guidelines

Areas	Recommendation	Use these lights
Counter and service area	High intensity lighting	Direct down lights or feature lighting that aligns with store branding
Perimeter lighting	Adds contrast to other store lighting and allows customers to read labeling and pricing easily on shelving fixtures	Pelmets with fluorescent lights shining on merchandise or halogens in the ceiling around the perimeter of the store
Display lighting	Should be different lighting from other areas	Track lighting can be placed above hot spot and entrance displays
Daylight	Too much daylight impedes the ability to control store ambiance and hinders varied lighting effects	Create your own ambience in-store rather than relying on daylight that you cannot control
Feature area lighting	Areas toward the rear of your store should be highlighted in order to invite customers to the rear	Halogen lights or powerful lighting features can be used Lamps or statement lights
Warehouse style stores with high ceilings	Lighting can be varied by installing areas with low ceilings	Trapeze halogen lighting suspended on wires is an option for stores with high ceilings and large feature lights can complement
Windows	Lighting should be focused onto merchandise	Discreet lighting that highlights message and merchandise

In summary, exceptional lighting is vitally important to enhance your exceptional brand statement. Investing in flooring and lighting will give you the best overall result in creating shopping environments that sell, especially in a small store and on a budget. Remember that the changing consumer has a higher expectation of shopping atmospherics and brands that deliver those expectations are more likely to engender customer loyalty.

Colours and finishes

Colour selection requires careful attention. Research says that consumers generally respond to colour in two ways, approach or avoidance.[80] Consumers can be attracted or repelled by good or bad use of colour. Early research from the 1980s outlines that the use of bright warm colours such as red and yellow on the exterior are most effective in drawing customers into the store and cool colours such as blue, purple and green are most effective to use for walls and displays.[81]

However, many of today's market leaders use bold lifestyle visuals and striking single colour brand statements on the exterior of their stores. Zara have massive images of target markets modeling merchandise over two story glass panels. Prada's Las Vegas City Center store uses huge two-storey LCD screens on a black background. Images are rotated on the screens to engage with consumers inside and outside the mall. Apple uses clear glass storefronts with no exterior colour statements, just the powerful Apple logo adorning the location. Woolworths use browns and naturals with green logos that send messages of earth, food and sustainability to their customers. The American hardware group Lowes, paint their stores in earth tones and adorn only their logo on the exterior of buildings to ensure the strongest possible brand statement.

In today's competitive retailscape, best practice applied to exterior colour schemes depends on your location and passing traffic. Standing out in the crowd with a message that connects with your target markets and reinforces your branding is the most effective strategy.

If your passing traffic is on foot, then powerful window displays with unique contemporary designs will most likely gain customer attention. If your passing trade is in motorcars travelling at 50 or 70 kilometres per hour, be bold with your exterior and ensure you make a unique brand statement to your target customers about your points of difference. Use your windows as billboards to tell your story. In today's modern culture, it is not the colours you choose so much as how relevant you make the use of those colours to connect with your target markets.

Fixtures

This is where I have seen retailers reuse, recycle and renovate ageing fixtures to save money and still align with their brand vision and personality. Recycling fixtures decreases your carbon footprint and costs less money adding to your environmental and economic sustainability. Slat walls and shelving can be repainted to breathe life into them once again.

For best results, avoid using too many contrasting finishes. Opt for the 'less is more' approach and eliminate anything that looks tired, aged or that the detailed eye sees as visually displeasing. Whatever you decide, it must align with your overall brand strategy and concept, connect with your new target markets and please your existing customers.

Ensure your fittings and fixtures are well designed to hold your stock. Many retailers have shelving and gondolas that do not display their stock in its best light and do not enable interactivity with the merchandise. Products behind glass sell less than products consumers can touch. Touching and trying the merchandise pre-purchase is pretty much the only point-of-difference to online selling, so it is best to promote it!

Visual merchandising will be made far easier if fixtures are well thought out and well designed, modular in nature and in a natural, basic black or white finish. Make sure you consult with a visual merchandiser when engaging your shop fitter to build fixtures that suit your merchandise and that align with your brand vision and personality.

If you spend most of your money on flooring and lighting to create an appealing environment, almost anything else will be 'forgiven' by your customers. If you don't create an appealing environment with these two elements, your brand personality cannot shine through and expensive finishes and fixtures will look average anyway. To be brutally honest, fluorescent lights and stark white slat walls from floor to ceiling just don't cut it any more!

Music

Music creates a mood and therefore adds to who you are and what you do. It is a powerful addition or detraction from the overall shopping and brand experience. Consideration must be given to the fact that playing music in your store constitutes public amplification of copyrighted materials. License agreements and fees apply in Australia through the Australian Performing Rights Association (APRA) and the Australasian Mechanical Copyright Owners Society (AMCOS). Whilst these organisations take a conservative approach to enforcing the copyright Act of 1968, legal action in extreme cases can be undertaken. Currently, licensing fees start from around AUD$70 per year for floor spaces under 150 square metres.[82]

In China, where policing the infringement of copyrighted music is a huge task, Lavaradio.com has eliminated licensing problems for retailers by providing tailor made radio playlists that can be amplified in stores in exchange for a small fee.

'Music played in a store can have a significant impact on a variety of behaviors including sales, arousal, perceptions of and actual time spent in the environment, in-store traffic flow, and the perception of visual stimuli in the retail store and the impact of music can be mediated by age of the shopper'.[83]

Music does impact how consumers shop in your environment therefore it can be used to positively or negatively impact your customers browsing and buying decisions. This should be carefully thought out and all customer segments considered when music playlists are created. Volume is an additional factor that adds or detracts from the shopping experience.

In Waikiki's shopping precinct in Honolulu, fashion store 'Guess' positioned a DJ in the window during an evening sales event. The music was at high volume. Customers flocked to the event, enjoying the music and the party atmosphere and merchandise flew off the racks. It was an entirely appropriate promotion for the brand's target market.

In the decade before the 2008 downturn, the Queensland based 'City Beach' group of stores executed sales events with in-store appearances by professional surfers and DJ's and skateboard ramp installations in some of their flagship stores. This style of experiential retailing was ground breaking in the Australian surf industry at the time and added to the brand enjoying 25 years of consecutive growth. These are all examples of retailers using music to enhance the shopping experience.

A note of warning! I have seen many parents walk out of guitar shops with their children and their money because a young sales assistant was playing his or her favourite death metal CD with the lyrics *'I hate my mother'* blaring throughout the store at unacceptable volumes. Interestingly, I have witnessed a few shopping centres in country regions playing classical music at entrance and exit points to ensure no loitering of unwanted young people takes place.

Consider which music is appropriate to your target segments and take care not to push any segments away if that is not your intention. It's best to have complete control over what music is played in your store and not rely on a radio station or an inexperienced staff member to choose the music.

Windows

Your window is the face of your brand and can be used to showcase 'the store's brands, styles, prices, and quality of the merchandise. Therefore, when looking at shop windows consumers search for clues about retailers' merchandise and promotional activities and for examples of the latest fashions and trends'.[84] Now that you have an insight into floor layout concepts, you will understand that placing your latest stock arrivals with healthy margin in the window is the best strategy to enhance your brand message and your profitability.

Over-filling windows with every category in the store and every product group on offer will send a message of low value and clutter to your customers. Attempting to showcase everything you stock in the window will likely have the opposite affect you were hoping for. An effective window display will persuade the customer to enter your store so it is a good idea to dual place the items in the window display inside your store for easy buying access.

A good rule to remember when merchandising windows is the more room you have around the merchandise, the higher the perceived value it will project to your customers. The visual merchandising section will go into more detail about *how* to merchandise your windows.

The in-store experience

The very latest global innovations that incorporate technology into store design in 2014 include holographic greeters, high-tech virtual mannequins, motion activated fittings,[85] interactive merchandising and windows, augmented fitting rooms and personalised shopping bags.[86]

Interaction is a key factor impacting on the consumer's overall shopping experience and **experiential retailing** is the new benchmark for market leaders. Retailers around the world such as Diesel, Nike, Vanquish, Luxottica, American Apparel and more are engaging in the fight to bring foot traffic back to bricks and mortar retail through designed experiences that are unique to their brands.

An example of experiential *design* can be found in a restaurant in Bali, Indonesia, called 'Potato Head Beach Club' (www.ptthead. com). *Now that's an experience!* A long driveway from the street has a checkpoint that sees guards inspect every vehicle to reassure patrons they are secure. On arrival there is one line for patrons who have made a booking and one for those who unfortunately, have not! Standing outside the enormous football stadium-like venue, patrons cannot see inside or hear any music. However, it is obvious by the size and contemporary design of the building that it is worth the wait to get in and so those who have not made a booking wait in anticipation.

There is a three storey high elliptical 'shield wall' made from window shutters on the outside of the building. This massive work of art makes a very clear promise to those waiting customers that the interior will also be a spectacular experience! It does the job of a shop window and storefront.

Finally, after twenty-five minutes waiting in the line and another security bag check, patrons are invited to enter in their parties. They walk along a curved entryway that is on the other side of the shield of shutters and are greeted by a seating waitress complete with head set and walkie-talkie that communicates with the front-of-house at all times.

The venue, designed by Indonesian architect Andra Matin, is absolutely stunning. The shutter theme is carried through the design in interesting and innovative ways and the artworks, furniture, finishes and impeccable workmanship provides a feast for the eyes. The amphitheatre style building fills with tourists and ex-pats in three large dining zones overlooking a massive grassed area so every single person bathes in a view of the amazing sunset that follows.

The food is gorgeous, drinks impeccable, service faultless and the DJ-led music adds to the overall amazing buzz that creates a relaxed party atmosphere. Staff hand patrons who have been relaxing in the pool fluffy white towels as they are seated for a casual and awesome dining experience. The restaurant is not expensive by world standards but the venue far exceeds anything seen Down Under.

The one-way exit flows into the retail store incorporating effective floor layout techniques similar to those used at IKEA. Tipsy customers are tempted to purchase high quality gifts and memorabilia and beautiful artworks that no doubt, have healthy margin attached. The venue has now embarked on building boutique accommodation to further enhance its revenue streams and economic sustainability.

Every detail of design has been thought through to enhance the Potato Head brand experience and connect with its ex-pat and tourist target markets. Patrons leave feeling thrilled, having enjoyed a stunning and memorable experience that is etched in their memories and talked about for a very long time afterwards. *It's a recipe for success!*

Creating a memorable in-store experience will enhance your brand and your foot traffic. How can you promise and deliver a memorable in-store experience to your customers on a smaller scale without huge investment? That is the challenge for you.

Presenting virtual tours and photo galleries of your in-store experience on your website and social media sites is a great way to showcase your brand's in-store point-of-difference from your competitors and can be a powerful way to engage with customers online in order to entice them to visit your store.

The online store experience

As I mentioned earlier, I believe it is no longer sustainable to exist as a bricks and mortar retailer selling across no other channels. Retailers that do not have a web presence risk being invisible to a wide audience that browse and purchase online. It is vital for specialty retailers to build a web presence through B2C (business to consumer) websites, blogs, social media platforms and m-commerce or mobile apps (applications). E-commerce websites start from around AUD$3000 or less and can now be built in very short time frames.

In the tiny New South Wales town of Cooma, an example of a specialty retailer who has excelled because of their online presence can be found. Birdsnest is a small retail boutique with a national customer base that has catapulted the business into massive growth through an excellent online strategy. The 'Birdsnest' website is exciting and unique, providing its point-of-difference by allowing customers to shop by colour, occasion or body shape.[87] In January 2014, the independent re-tail store had an amazing 54,000 'Likes' on Facebook growing at a rate of approximately 4000 per month, and 1500 Twitter followers!

Birdsnest attaches a card to its merchandise with a nice message to each customer, further enhancing the personal brand experience. I believe customers do want to shop locally and will shop online from local stores if the offer is compelling and competitive. Wouldn't you rather shop from a domestic website than overseas?

All of these store design elements are vehicles that will help you communicate your brand meaning. You can now go ahead with confidence, be bold and brave and **sass up your store design** to stand out and make a fabulous first impression on your customers!

Body boards online

In 2010, Cher owned a small group of body board and surfwear stores. One day I popped in to see how she was going. We started talking about online selling and how her website was doing. To my surprise, Cher told me that most of her online sales were from locals and some of them were from customers who lived literally within walking distance who wanted home delivery. Online is all about convenience and connecting with your customers the way they shop. Cher was onto it way back then! **Consider your B2C website as a relevant and convenient way customers can buy from you**

Quick Tips to sass-up your store design

1. **Connect** with your target audience through your store design
2. **Redesign** your store to make a statement aligning with your brand vision and core values outlining who you are and what you do
3. **Incorporate** innovation, interaction and sustainability in your design, shop fit and materials
4. **Create** ambience for your retail brand through flooring and lighting
5. **Update** your store every 4-5 years
6. **Ensure** your fixtures are modular and well designed
7. **Consider** merchandising applications when shop fitting and designing
8. **Control** the music you play
9. **Utilise** your windows to make a strong statement
10. **Incorporate** an online store element and experience to your RBM

Secret 17-Modify your merchandise assortment

The product brands, breadth and depth of range, private labels and price points that you choose to stock make up your **merchandise assortment**. What you carry can be your point of differentiation from your competitors and can help give you a competitive advantage. The breadth of your merchandise assortment refers to the number of product lines carried and the depth refers to the brands, models, styles, colours and sizes in your range.[88]

'Consumers perceptions of the depth of a retailer's assortment within a product category are an important dimension of store image and a key driver of store choice. Greater perceived assortment does influence store image, store choice and satisfaction, but a greater number of SKUs (stock keeping units or product items) need not directly translate to better perceptions. Retailers *can* reduce the number of SKUs substantially without adversely affecting consumer perceptions, as long as they pay attention to the most preferred brands'.[89]

Consumers want choice so they can make comparisons and purchase decisions but there is no need to stock everything across product ranges. Additionally, specialty retailers do not have the room nor the resources to stock wide and deep product ranges that equal their competitors and so must consider making careful buying choices based on consumer driven tastes, trends and stock turns to ensure purchasing decisions are the right ones.

Peter Ryan, well respected head of Red Communications, a Sydney based retail strategy consultancy, recently said 'Customers are now actively looking for uniqueness, great stories, quality, attention to detail and engagement. It is most attractive when it is product led. That is the era we are now confronting.'[90]

Expanding product ranges through giving customers access to online purchasing whilst in-store is an interactive way that specialty retailers can add greater breadth and depth to ranges to satisfy customer needs without over capitalising on stock.

The most crucial step to achieving effective product assortment is definitely when you choose your range and buy your stock. Buying the right stock in the right quantities at the right time is a difficult formula for any retailer to get right every time and so requires careful consideration. A balanced approach is to examine customer preferences, brand equity or brand 'pull' into your store, supplier relationships, private label opportunities (direct supply), supply chains, cash flow, margins and the ability to compete in the marketplace.

Revising brands

The notion of 'brand portfolio' refers to the product brands you choose to stock. Known or high equity brands can be a primary reason for consumers to visit your store and probably make up the bulk of your portfolio. Revising your brand strategy can help to diversify your business model and your suppliers. Partnering with multiple suppliers allows you to avoid putting all your eggs in one basket and gives you the flexibility to adapt when changes in the marketplace occur. If you have too many suppliers, consolidation can save you both time and money.

Supplier relationships are of course essential to your business, so changes to brand stocking can be tricky to navigate, especially when looking to incorporate private label products through shorter supply chains that provide bigger margins for you. In short, the introduction of private labels requires careful consideration and planning.

Unfortunately, this is a pressing issue as it becomes increasingly difficult for specialty retailers to compete with market leaders when selling high equity manufacturer product brands. Buying power, rebates and vertical models available to market leaders are all adding to the pressure independents face in today's marketplace.

Stocking your own private label brand can represent a supplementary product range that diversifies your margin and supply. The quality of manufacturer brands you stock positively influences the consumer's image of your store brand and improves the perceived value of your own private label brand.[91]

Manufacturer or national brands help to create and enhance your retail image and can build customer loyalty, but sometimes represent unsustainable margins for specialty retailers. Essentially, a large portion of most specialty retailer's profit comes from the manufacturer brands they choose to stock and generic or private label merchandise can serve as extra margin that adds to overall RBM sustainability.

National brands help sell private labels

> As a visual merchandising manager for a specialty retail chain, I embarked on a program to place a private label brand next to a national brand leader in one category in all 120 stores. After the first year of this new placement strategy there was a national increase in sales of the private label of 10% and the second year 11%. This represented a substantial increase in turnover and profit margin across the group and was at a time when markets were flat. **Placing your private label products next to market-leading brands maximises category profit**[92]

Two brands are better than one

> When selling-in a keyboard range to retailers against his direct brand competitors, Geoff, a National brand manager for Casio said 'If you stock my brand *and* my competitor's brand, I promise you will sell more of both!' That was his brand promise to his customers and he was right. Casio keyboards built and grew a successful Australian distribution network based on that promise. **Consumers want to be able to choose between competing brands in one location**

The best buying strategy and that used by market leaders is to combine manufacturer brands and private label brands into the merchandise assortment mix in order to improve overall margin. The pie chart below shows a diversified approach to brands and margins.

Diversified margin approach

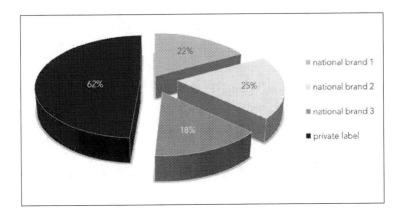

Brand performance

As I have discussed previously, a great way to think about your shop floor is by considering dollar return on investment per square metre. After all, that's how your rent is calculated. Brands can also be measured taking this approach. Your brand preferences, stock purchasing and placement decisions ought to be based on this economical rationale including sales volume and margin for best results.

Here's how to measure your product brands in terms of return on investment (ROI) per square metre. Let's say you sell a total of $150,000 of brand X per year and your margin is 22%= $33,000 profit. Your cost to buy the goods is $117,000. The space the brand takes up is 5m2 in each store x 10 stores=50m2. Now let's divide $33,000 (your profit) by 50m (total space)=$660 per square metre. $660 per square metre x 50 metres. Therefore, annual sales=$3000 per square meter per annum. How much is your rent per square metre per annum? (Divide your annual rent by your total floor metreage). How much are your overhead costs per square metre? The answer will tell you if you need to make an adjustment up or down for floor space for this brand.

Calculating this equation will give you a better idea of how much floor space to dedicate to each brand in your portfolio. It is always a good idea to give more space to your brands that have higher margins and to take a balanced but informed approach to decision making.

Buying and consigning

Stock purchasing must be based on what your customers want and what sells best according to sales histories and consumer demand. Looking to your competitors and partners to understand trends and gain information about your sector is vital to help you make the best buying decisions. Industry, Government reports and Association websites are a great place to look for market information and suppliers often have easy access to what's selling and what's not.

Visiting your market leading stores with *your BIG on* is also a good way to stay on top of what products and price points are in demand and which products are being dumped in your marketplace due to poor sales or low demand. It's worth considering a simple buying structure for your business that outlines a buying budget. This may stop your store from overspending in any given month and keep cash flows under check. Plan for all aspects of your buying taking into account your customers, representatives, storage, margins, stock turns, packaging and merchandising.

Review your suppliers for the best buying deals remembering that you almost certainly buy at a disadvantage to your competitors.

It's pretty safe to say that your suppliers can always sell cheaper to you than what they offer. Negotiate hard on buy prices and re-buy prices with your existing and new suppliers. Take advantage of settlement discounts as they can make a difference to your bottom line. Make sure you negotiate the best deals on shipping and handling and use your own couriers and insurers if there is a cost benefit.

Be vigilant about getting credits in order quickly. Use histories to forecast sales taking into account market trends and purchase quantities. Try not to let representatives talk you into buying excessive volumes of stock just to get 'the deal'. The aim is not to be left with 20% of your stock that you have to mark down to sell at no profit. This is where most of your end profit will lie and you don't want your money tied up in dead stock that won't sell.

Consigning or putting in a range of stock from your suppliers and paying for it as it sells, is a great way to improve cash flows and reduces the cost of overstocks or stock that is not moving. Ask your suppliers if they have this option. More and more suppliers are willing to do this as business conditions toughen and shorter supply chains threaten their future. Ask your suppliers for help with advertising, merchandising, point-of-sale materials and any other resources they may have to help you sell more of their products.

Scarcity tactic

Fashion retailer Zara uses the scarcity tactic in its merchandise assortment strategy. Stores receive limited amounts of stock knowing they will sell out quickly. This tactic reduces the amount of overstocks and thus the need for markdowns. Consumers learn that there are limited styles for short periods of time and buy now rather than later. 'Zara can design, produce, and deliver a new garment and put it on display in its stores worldwide in a mere 15 days. Such a pace is unheard of in the fashion business, where designers typically spend months planning for the next season. Because Zara can offer a large variety of the latest designs quickly and in limited quantities, it collects 85% of the full ticket price on its retail clothing, while the industry average is 60% to 70%. As a result, it achieves a higher net margin on sales than its competitors.'[93] **Good buying is a balancing act between no out-of-stocks and no overstocks!**

Quick Tips to modify your merchandise assortment

1. **Diversify** your merchandise mix and brand mix so you have flexibility
2. **Ensure** your overall average margin is sustainable
3. **Look at** introducing a portion of your own sourced private label with a higher margin if possible or shortening the supply chain to retain margin
4. **Negotiate** with all your suppliers for better buying conditions
5. **Avoid** overbuying and look to the market for what to buy

Secret 18-Rev-up your visual merchandising

Visual merchandising (VM) is the presentation of store advertising, special events, new product and dressing of departments, fixtures and windows to create shopping environments to enhance the sale of goods and services offered by your outlet. Merchandise should always be displayed in its best light to show off features and benefits to the customer. The purpose of VM is to 'attract, engage and motivate the customer towards making a purchase'.[94]

As a young sales representative, I found that whenever I merchandised products in a store, surprise, surprise, they sold out and my customers reordered quicker, adding to my sales figures and my back pocket! It may seem obvious that good merchandising really works but many retailers do not give it priority and so do not maximise sales for their stores. VM is the single most powerful silent sales tool and goes hand-in-hand with personal selling.

Creating displays that sell

Consumers differ in their selection behaviours and so it is important to incorporate several different display types in your store to maximise sales opportunities. For example, some consumers like to buy from *product category displays*. This is where you have products grouped together in a product category to display your range of merchandise. A wall of 'glassware' in a homewares store is a product category display. A shelving display of 'interior paint' brands in a paint outlet is a product category display and an area dedicated to 'acoustic guitars' in a music shop is a product category display. The best position for category displays is on wall fixtures around the store.

Other consumers like to buy from *hotspot displays* placed strategically around the store. These displays incorporate full margin lines and promotional price offers on high volumes of stock. For example, in front or adjacent to the glassware category, you may have a floor stack of a '6 box set of glasses' at $19.95. You may build a high margin floor stack of '10 litre low sheen' near the interior paint category priced at $125.00 or you might have a stack of 'solid top acoustic guitars' priced at $295 in the middle of the acoustic guitar category.

Some consumers see the hotspot displays but miss the category display or vice versa, so it is always important to include hotspot merchandise in the product category display on the shelf, in its range, at the promotional price and highlighted with a price ticket. This way you can avoid missing any sales opportunities.

Arranging products of the same colour group together is visually effective and widely used in fashion and homeware outlets. This strategy, known as *colour blocking,* helps eliminate clutter and allows consumers to shop with colour as their first preference. Using this technique means that product categories are mixed together and so your revised categories become *colour* categories instead of *product* categories.

Cross-merchandised displays place products from differing categories together that may not necessarily be colour blocked. These products usually have a high likelihood of being sold together if placed with one another. For example, a leading liquor chain places mixer soft drinks right next to spirits on the shelf in the spirits category. Tonic water is placed next to gin and Coca Cola next to bourbon whiskey. Employing this strategy allows the store to silently and suggestively sell these products to self-serving customers.

This tactic increases the average sale through add-on purchasing because customers conveniently buy both spirits and mixers from the same fixture at the same time. The mixer drinks are also available in the mixer drinks category in the store and so this strategy can also be termed *dual placement.*

The same product can appear in several locations around the store depending on cross-merchandising opportunities, relationships between products and consumer buying psychology and behaviours. Another example of effective cross-merchandising is when supermarkets place pasta sauce with pasta in a floor stack in the veggie section right next to tomatoes or near the cheese fridge. *You can't miss it and you buy more!*

Price-point displays are where products at the same price are grouped together to sell the value aspect of the goods. This is where price is highlighted as the consumer buying focus. CD and video stores commonly used this strategy before iTunes made their business irrelevant and many continue to close their doors. However, this is an effective display type to use during a sale event and is commonly used in Kmart, Target, Walmart and Costco.

Lifestyle displays are aimed at showcasing products and putting them into context with how they will enrich your customer's lives. These displays are often in windows and incorporate props that enhance the merchandise. Market leaders show the product in its best light and entice the consumer to buy from an emotional 'must-have' perspective.

Furniture and homeware retailers Freedom and IKEA, are adept at presenting their stock in lifestyle displays because their range of products lends itself to this display type. These retailers create entire apartments using lifestyle displays to showcase their products, which cross multiple product categories.

These brands also incorporate product category displays for ease of selection and product comparison. For example, chairs, rugs, bedding, lighting and so on are merchandised in product categories in addition to room lifestyle displays. A mixture of display types is the best way to enhance the shopping experience for your customers and provides an interesting and engaging encounter that maximises sales.

IKEA is one of the world's most successful retail brands. A ground breaking and contemporary merchandising strategy that was developed by the organisation and used today by many successful retailers is known by the catch phrase '*I can see, I can buy.*' Essentially, these displays represent fast and efficient volume-selling opportunities.

Displays showcase merchandise above eye level or within consumer reach to see, touch, feel and try. All relevant information is outlined on items including price, features, benefits, measurements etc, and a volume stack or basket of available stock for purchase is placed below the display so consumers can help themselves.

This strategy enables the CBP (consumer buying process) to occur by providing all necessary information to allow customers to make buying decisions on the spot. All buying objections are overcome through providing adequate information to the browsing consumer. It also minimises the number of staff floor-walkers needed on hand. The retailer is able to achieve lower running costs adding to the bottom line.

The consumer simply looks at, touches or tries the item, reaches over and picks one up in new packaging. *'I can see, I can buy'* is the ultimate VM tool for maximising fast and efficient sales volume and is a strategy that can easily be incorporated into your store today.

Window displays often sell a lifestyle promise and the primary job of your windows is to get customers to enter your store. There are several important elements to creating impactful window displays that look professional and that sell. This section will appeal to the *artiste* inside you! Window displays with excellent composition incorporate balance, harmony, proportion, balance, rhythm, uniformity and the pyramid.

Balance can be explained in two forms. Symmetry is a centred and equal balance and asymmetry is an off-centre or unequal balance. Equal quantities of merchandise are incorporated in a symmetrical display that will have a traditional or mirror-like look and feel. The use of asymmetry will project a contemporary or cutting-edge look and feel through the placement of merchandise into an uneven yet pleasing-to-the-eye balanced arrangement.

Harmony is the agreement amongst the elements of design, colour and texture of your display. As a starting point, it's easiest to stick with three colours and one texture to ensure your display does not look cluttered or project a message of low value.

Emphasis is the centre of attraction of your display, which should always be the merchandise. Your overall display design should make what you are selling obvious.

Proportion is a very important element when building professional looking displays that sell. One object should not seem too large or too small in proportion to the rest.

The rules of proportion are those based on Leonardo Da Vinci's c1490 drawing of the 'Vetruvian man' depicting the perfect proportions of man and the universe and named after ancient Roman architect Vitruvius.

Objects should be in proportion to each other using the 1/3 or 2/3 rule. Imagine a painting on a wall. In order to follow the rules of proportion, it should be 1/3 or 2/3 the size of the wall in order for it to be in proportion with the space in which it is hung. This is a reason why many people experience difficulty when furnishing their homes without design advice. The decorating novice may not be aware that furniture objects must be in proportion to the size of the room and rugs in proportion to floor space, cushions in proportion to lounges, paintings in proportion to wall space and so on.

A general decorating rule called 60, 30, 10 outlines that 60% of any given area should be the overall colour, 30 percent for flooring and furniture and 10 percent trims, pillows, rugs and accessories. Architects and artists use this rule as a foundation for their work and designers break all the rules once they are accomplished and brave enough to create a style or look of their own!

Rhythm can be used in displays to lead the eyes of the consumer throughout the entire display. Visual merchandisers often scatter small objects or add rhythmic elements to capture interest from the observing audience. For example, contemporary displays often have many items hanging from the ceiling to create rhythm.

Uniformity is of critical importance. Using uniform angles to line products up with precision allows merchandise to be seen clearly and minimises clutter, which is more pleasing to the eye. This makes the merchandise look more valuable and so aids in value enhancing it. When uniformity is incorporated in displaying items, housekeeping standards are highlighted and often improved as a consequence.

Use of the *pyramid* helps achieve sound composition for your display. Begin with the largest object at the back and work your way down in size to the smallest. Create pyramids within pyramids, grouping items and overlapping them to tie the display together to create flow throughout your display. Ignoring the pyramid element will generally result in items being spread out over the available display space and will create 'negative spaces' in your display that stand out more than the merchandise. This will detract from the professional look and feel that market leaders achieve.

Risers are used to lift your merchandise off the floor in your windows or in stand-alone store displays. Lifting your displays to eye level hotspot positioning and up off the floor will aid in improving the perceived overall value of the goods. The use of risers such as plinths, boxes, chairs, tables or anything that compliments the merchandise helps to create a story about your stock and can be used to add interest to your display.

Props should be used with care in window displays and never be the centre of attention. If your window looks like you are selling the props you have used, you may need to review how you have incorporated emphasis in your display. The merchandise or brand message should always be the focus of effective window displays.

There is no need to pricemark stock in the window unless you are tying in a promotion where price is an important element. All of these rules and more can and have been broken by professional visual merchandisers who create artistic and impactful displays, just like artists who create original paintings. However, if you are just discovering these principles, its best to follow these basic rules for guaranteed success with **creating displays that sell.**

Many specialty retailers view building window displays as the most subordinate task in the day-to-day running of the store and generally delegate it to the most inexperienced staff member with limited visual merchandising expertise. Yet this task is responsible for sending the right message to the right customers by showcasing what you have to offer in the very best possible way. It requires skill and careful consideration to execute effectively. If you think you do not have the skills or resources to build impactful and interesting displays that incorporate *balance, harmony, emphasis, proportion, rhythm, uniformity and the pyramid*, engage a professional window dresser or VM to help you.

If you need visual stimulation to help your creative juices, there are literally millions of photographs available online. Google 'window displays', click on 'images' and you have an instant array of captivating windows at your fingertips. You can even type in your favourite retailer to see inspirational windows from all over the world. *Try it!*

Here is a simple diagram that outlines how the primary principles discussed in this section come together when creating displays that sell. *Have fun!*

Visual merchandising display principles

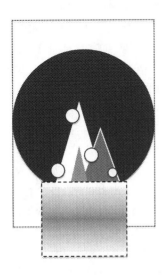

1. Balance: Display is well balanced through symmetry or asymmetry
2. Harmony: Not too many colours or textures
3. Emphasis: Is the merchandise
4. Proportion: Composition and objects are 1/3 or 2/3 size
5. Rhythm: Small white and black circles lead the eyes through the display
6. Uniformity: All components are facing the same way
7. Pyramid: Incorporation of triangles within triangles
   • Grouping: Merchandise is grouped together
   • Overlap: All components are overlapping with others to avoid negative space

Shelf management

Shelf layout, range, size, refilling and price ticketing are all part of retail **shelf management** strategy. Market leaders use visual maps known as planograms to help plan every square centimetre of fixture layouts. Planograms are the visual communication vehicle used to implement merchandising strategies that maximise profits. They provide a visual guide for product placement on fixtures so merchandising can be simultaneously implemented quickly, effectively and uniformly across many stores.

Planograms consider brand, size, price, margin and labeling and are generally created by merchandise managers, suppliers or by collaboration between both. As a single store retailer, there is no need to planogram your fixture layouts. However, it is important to be aware of how and why they work and to consider incorporating some of their advantages into your shelf management practices.

There are many advantages to using planograms in medium to large retail chains. Planograms help achieve a balance between consumer demand and shelf inventory demonstrating appropriate stock holding quantities and delivering lower costs. Out-of-stocks reduce as ranging is clearly defined and sales rates are monitored closely leading to more revenue and better customer satisfaction.

Planograms incorporate vertical brand blocking leading to better brand representation with guaranteed product placement for suppliers, and improved relationships with trading partners. Planogrammed shelf layouts stimulate desired purchasing behaviour from consumers adding to overall revenue and profitability.

Planning and implementation of shelf layouts across multiple stores creates a consistent national brand and marketing message leading to better customer satisfaction, visual appeal, higher brand loyalty and increased sales. Planograms lead to improved usage of retail space translating to a higher return on investment per square centimetre.

Finally, planograms enable better communication and more efficient use of staff time during shelf merchandising relays amounting to lower costs and less disruption for customers during trading hours.

An example amongst retailers who incorporate placement of highest margin and highest volume product lines into best positions through planogram planning is 'The Body Shop'. The Body Butter range represents the brand's highest volume and highest margin product line and so takes precedence in all hotspot locations in-store. The product is merchandised in several different ways.

Some displays incorporate colour blocking and product stories, and others show the entire body butter product breadth and depth of assortment in one section. A skilled merchandise manager creates the best layout for shelving displays and photographs or planograms are sent to all stores for quick and effective implementation. Planograms are dynamic and are designed with profit in mind.

Leading hardware retailers are among those who employ planograms and a size positioning strategy in their shelf layouts. For example, one-litre paint tins, which have the highest margin are placed in the eye level zone and the less profitable but higher dollar value four-litre tins, are placed below and above eye level in warmer zones.

One of today's leading Australian and American owned paint retailers have taken this strategy a step further and de-ranged two-litre sizes of paint altogether for most brands, silently persuading consumers to purchase more of what the retailer would most like to sell, enhancing profitability.

The consumer is often unaware of these types of shelf management approaches and simply purchase from the choice on offer. When small changes aimed at increasing profits are incorporated into shelf layouts across large retail chains, the result can amount to increases of many hundreds of thousands of dollars. In a small specialty store environment, incorporating some of these strategies that planograms enable can increase sales and profitability dramatically.

Planograms regularly change as products are deleted, discontinued, de-ranged or re-priced. In large retailers, national brands are often positioned within planogram layouts in premium hot spot eye level positions in exchange for a fee, as are primary hotspot floor locations as previously mentioned. Brand merchandisers visit supermarkets on a weekly call cycle to try to secure unpaid additional hotspot product displays around stores in order to increase national sales of their brands.

This fact demonstrates how important hotspot locations are and reinforces them as the most valuable real estate in your store. Hotspots can be used to leverage advantages with suppliers, even if it is only a buy price discount. Entrance areas, counters, gondola ends and eye level zones are your most effective silent selling positions. Consider that when you can guarantee your suppliers that the hotspots in your store are merchandised in a timely and effective way, they can be used as a bargaining tool to make gains when buying stock. *Try it!*

In summary, the most useful information for specialty retailers about planograms is that products placed in the eye level zone will be more exposed to customers and so placing highest margin where possible in those zones will positively impact profitability. If shelf management and hotspot positioning practices are effective and efficient, charging a fee for product placement is not out of the question and represents a further way towards competitiveness and sustainability for specialty retailers.

Vertical blocking

Incorporating **vertical blocking** by brand grouping or by colour grouping is a visually impactful and effective tactic used by market leaders. If stock is merchandised into a portrait rectangular block from left to right and top to bottom it makes sense to the western consumer, like reading a book. This layout is also the most pleasing to the eye.

Vertical blocking by brand can be advantageous to stores that stock multiple brands ensuring eye level and hotspot real estate is shared across all brands with varying margins. This is particularly helpful to those stores that do not have a private or generic brand available to them. Vertical brand blocking gives brands a strong in-store footprint, which keeps your suppliers happy and adds brand strength to each individual product brand.

Negative space

When you run out of a stock item and the shelf has an empty space, it leaves behind a **negative space**, which has a number of undesirable consequences. Your store cannot sell an out-of-stock item therefore it is lost revenue forever. It sends a message to your customers that you cannot afford to stock your store so you are going out of business or you are not able to manage your stock well.

Often, specialty retailers say to me, 'Oh, it's the end of the month, so there are gaps on the shelf'. Do consumers buy more at the beginning of the month than at the end? The consumer just wants to buy an item that is in stock, all the time, regardless of the day of the month. I have seen many retailers achieve their budgets because their shelves were full at the end of the month and seen many fall short because their shelves were empty. Do your market leading competitors have gaps on their shelves at the end of the month? The practice of running down stock at month's end can represent lost sales revenue and more adversely, lost consumer loyalty.

Ask your suppliers for longer trading terms if you need more time to pay instead of exposing yourself to the consequences of negative space. Remember the 'No Frills' chain with their constantly half empty shelves that looked like a Russian supermarket during the cold war? Consumers got sick of out-of-stocks and moved on to other supermarket brands, adding to the demise of the business model in Australia.

Out-of-stocks inconvenience your customers and so they are more likely to go to one of your competitors for what they need.

If you are out-of-stock of a 'bread and butter' line, consumers may seek to change their buying habits and search online for alternatives. Today's savvy consumer may attempt to interrupt your supply chain and buy directly from an online supplier, cutting you out of the supply chain altogether as a result. The cost to the business for an out-of-stock is far greater than one lost sale. It could be the lifetime value of a customer that is lost due to an out-of-stock situation.

Out-of-stocks are sometimes unavoidable due to a link in the supply chain failing. In this situation if it's feasible, place an alternative product in the negative space that will do the same job in order to protect the sale and keep the customer happy. Be sure to change the price if applicable. Do everything you can to *keep the customer happy and loyal!*

Another strategy to avoid negative space is to 'face-up' or 'double-face' the stock you *do* have to fill the empty spaces of the stock you don't have. Stock should always be pulled to the front and labels turned to the front, faced up for the next set of eyes that are expecting to see the product in its best light. It's appropriate that store personnel are all considered responsible for the daily and sometimes hourly facing-up of stock.

It's important to note that employing the scarcity tactic that we discussed earlier with global fashion chain Zara, versus having negative space on shelving are two very different scenarios. Scarcity can be used to make consumers buy items that have a limited shelf lifetime whereas negative spaces are ongoing lines that are not available and leave an empty space on the shelf.

The good bits are gone!

A chemist inside a hospital had a slat wall display of nuts, dried fruits and health food bars. There were many lines out-of-stock that created multiple negative spaces (I call that negative clutter). I asked Natalie, the store manager, what happened to the wall. She said, 'The nurses have come down from the hospital and bought all the good bits. The one's left are not selling and we can't reorder for another two weeks as we have no open-to-buy'. I said 'Yes, it looks exactly like all the good bits are gone and only the bad ones are left!' I showed Nat and her staff how to relay the slat wall into a vertical block and spread out the stock giving extra facings to lines that had duplicates to make the wall look full and fresh again. After 7 days and before the stock reorder, I returned to see what had transpired. Three quarters of the apparent non-saleable lines had sold and the slat wall was once again full of negative space! **Negative space requires constant attention for each set of new customer eyes**

Facings

The number of same items you have grouped together on the shelf is called product **facings**. For example, you may have five facings of the same product on the shelf for a few reasons. Firstly, you sell more of that item than others and five facings merchandised four deep on the shelf represents 4-6 weeks of sales of that product for your store.

This ensures that you never run out of stock and never endure the effects of negative space. Secondly, you may want to sell more of that particular product because you are holding more stock or it has a higher margin than other stock. Adding extra facings of these lines to the fixture will maximise your sales of higher profit.

Interestingly, it works both ways with consumers and facings. What I mean is, if the demand for a product is high, it requires more facings to avoid out-of-stocks and if a product has more facings, consumers naturally think the item must be popular and so are more likely to buy it. Facings are a chicken and egg relationship so it is important that you reassess your shelf layouts to constantly improve your range, sales and margin as a way to enhance your overall profitability therefore adding to your economic sustainability.

Ticketing

If price consideration is part of the consumers buying process, then pricing on all items is best practice. Have you ever looked at an item with no price on it? What is your natural reaction? You put it down and walk away because you can't make your decision to buy it without first knowing the price. Is it free? Or is it overpriced? If it is not free and it is not overpriced, why does it not have a price displayed on it?

Asking for the price makes most consumers feel uncomfortable. Why would a retailer make their valuable customers feel uncomfortable during their buying process? Pricing is a basic customer service that must be incorporated into your store's RBM. No market leaders in the world neglect price marking. In fact, in some large US retail chains, no price on an item can mean instant dismissal for the manager who missed it! *That's tough!*

I frequently hear objections about pricing like 'It's too much work' or 'Prices are changing soon anyway' or 'I want the customer to talk to me first so I can sell to them'. These are all outdated reasons for not price marking merchandise. Pricing can be a mammoth task if you have a large store, but it will improve sales immediately due to more customers able to finalise their buying decisions at no cost to the business.

Perhaps the reason that some retailers do not price is they are trying to get the highest possible price for goods by selling at RRP or inflating the price and then discounting to create the illusion of a bargain for their customers? Remember that consumers have embraced mobile commerce and in 2011 an estimated 48% of consumers price checked using their mobile devices.[95] Price transparency is now unavoidable.

Paint shop sees the price light

Graham was resisting adding prices to his merchandise for years. After my visit, he could see the opportunities he was missing out on and got to price marking all of his stock. He insists to this day that price marking his stock improved sales by 20% overnight! **Price marking merchandise is an expectation of today's consumer and increases fast and efficient sales**

Price tickets should be uniform across the store to minimise clutter. Market leaders incorporate several different ticket types including shelf talkers, A4 and A5 size and varying tailor made sizes to display neat, clear and relevant price tickets with adequate information for consumers to make purchase decisions. Always consider that a hand written ticket is better than no ticket and that consumer pricing laws apply to price ticketing.[96]

Airport hurry!

It never ceases to amaze me that I can still find a store in a capital city airport that has no price tickets at all on impulse items! Consumers at airports often make hasty buying decisions and do not have time to ask an attendant the price. No price represents an inconvenience for your customers. **Price all of your impulse lines clearly for highest volumes of sales**

The buying process ignored

Recently, Rosita and I visited a sporting goods store that has existed for 30 years. On entering, she proclaimed 'Oh my god this store is hurting my eyes, it's a total sensory overload'. We couldn't find the women's wear department and we felt unsafe walking on the wobbly gangway stairs. The change rooms were round rails with flimsy curtains that we determined very quickly would not be private enough for us to try anything on. When we were browsing, we saw some trolley wheels for stand-up-paddleboards (SUP). Rosita desperately wanted one and had been looking for months. The store had a range of around 10 different styles, which she was excited about. Excitement turned to despair when there were no prices on anything. The store was running on skeleton staff two weeks before Christmas. Finally, after waiting to ask the price for 15 minutes, she walked out feeling disappointed that she was empty-handed and had to continue to carry her SUP to the beach. She was ready to part with up to $200 for her trolley but she needed to see the prices in order to make a buying decision. We never told the store they lost her money, we just left after waiting too long to ask a simple pricing question that could have been answered by a little white sticker! **You may never know how many customers you have lost by not pricing products. If a customer walks out quickly after looking at an item, I bet it had no price on it!**

Housekeeping

Integrated **housekeeping** policies are essential to maintain high retail presentation standards but are often not given adequate attention. Store frontage, gardens, windows, flooring, fixtures, counters, stock, restrooms and staff presentation all add to or detract from the consumers first impression and the overall shopping experience in your store. These elements require constant attention to remain at the highest possible standard and should be monitored closely.

When it comes to stock, it's all about the consumer's *perception* that they are the first person to pick up a product or try on a garment that is 'brand new'. The presentation or restoration of stock to 'as new' condition after a consumer has tested or tried it on, is called *stock recovery*. This means that stock that has been touched, moved or tried by consumers is constantly managed back to new status. Realistically, many consumers may have tried a product before your store actually sells it, so it is important that stock items are recovered for each new customer.

Leading fashion retailers iron, button, zip and beautifully rehang garments after each person has tried the items. Fashion store personnel are constantly folding, hanging and fussing over individual garments in order to give the next customer the impression that stock is brand new. During sale periods, leading fashion retailers including Zara, roster additional staff hours to ensure quick recovery of garments, which aids in achieving the best possible result from sale events.

Standard consumer behaviour is to pull goods out of packaging, touch and feel, perhaps even try and then search for a new one in brand new packaging, even though the packaging is thrown in the bin the moment it is opened at home. *Crazy humans!*

IKEA use the *I can see, I can buy* strategy to enable this behaviour by displaying each item out of its packaging so customers *can* see, touch, feel, smell and test before they pick up a new one in a box to take to the checkout. The damage caused to the sample stock by consumers trying it is seen by IKEA and other market leaders, as a cost of doing business (COB) and sample stocks are replaced when they begin to look used. Damaged and handled stock is sent to the run-out destination section, which is positioned adjacent to the checkouts.

Displaying one item and keeping the rest in packaging is the best strategy for specialty retailers to follow when selling multiples of the same stock. If you sell one-off products such as expensive guitars or individual wedding dresses for example, the consumer's perception must be that the item is new, even if it has had two birthdays in your store and fifty people have tried it. Therefore, stock recovery is important to ensure your stock remains looking, smelling and feeling brand new.

Unless you actually sell second hand goods, it's best to remove items from your store that do not appear to be new. Consumers will not buy used or damaged items at full price and their visibility in-store lowers the perceived value of the rest of your stock. Display items via the *I can see, I can buy* method and when goods become used sell them on Gumtree or Ebay as second hand. You will probably still get more than you paid for these items, turning stock into cash, and you won't risk sending the wrong message to your customers that your stock is second hand.

Eliminate any soiled or damaged stock from your showroom and turf out any damaged packaging. Looking after your stock daily will ensure it remains in as-new condition. That means housekeeping chores are a priority. Polishing guitars daily, changing the strings every week if necessary and dry cleaning dresses after five people have tried them on and left make-up marks on them, is essential. How many times does a car yard detail its cars before they are sold as new?

Refilling and rotating stock regularly is an important part of shelf management to minimise out-of-stocks and keep stock looking fresh and new. Ensure that old labeling is sold first or replaced and soiled or damaged stock is removed from fixtures altogether.

It is extra work to keep all stock items in new condition but the key is to clean, dust and polish stock every day. Glass windows and cabinets should be cleaned to avoid finger marks and smudges. Floors vacuumed or mopped daily. Consumers don't want to buy dirty or dusty stock or be exposed to a dirty or dusty environment. Ask yourself 'Would I buy this stock for my wife or husband in this condition?' *After all, retail is detail!*

To end this section (pun intended), a quick note about housekeeping and restrooms. Market leaders provide restrooms as a convenience for customers to make the shopping experience more enjoyable. Customers cannot continue to shop when nature calls! If you have a restroom in your store, allow customers to use the facilities and clean them several times a day. After all, using a restroom is a basic human right by all accounts. Even if a person wishes to use your restroom and is not your customer today, they must really need to use it if they have come in off the street in the hope of finding yours!

Consider that tomorrow, they may be your customers and if you refuse them, that potential business will dissolve. Restrooms, when used by the general public and your customers must be clean, well stocked and free from occupational health and safety dangers such as ladders or stock in cartons.

Defining and communicating housekeeping standards through a checklist tool is the best way to achieve and maintain tip-top housekeeping in your organisation.

Quick Tips to rev-up your visual merchandising

1. **Use** different display types to engage with different customers
2. **Focus** on hotspot control around the store
3. **Maximise** colour blocking and vertical blocking techniques
4. **Incorporate** balance, harmony, emphasis, proportion, rhythm, uniformity, the pyramid, overlap and flow in window displays
5. **Use** 'I can see, I can buy' as a powerful volume seller
6. **Avoid** negative space like the plague
7. **Consider** stock turns, margin, facings and vertical blocking when incorporating shelf management strategies
8. **Price** ticket all products to enable the buying decisions and the CBP
9. **Attend** to housekeeping and recovery as a priority

Secret 19-Prepare your pricing plan

Advising retailers on pricing strategies that directly affect margin and profit is often 'tricky' like talking about religion and politics! However, the fact remains that many specialty retailers do not have a formal pricing structure or strategy in place and so tend to work on an ad-hoc basis dealing with pricing issues as they arise. Leading retailers incorporate very specific pricing structures and policies that set the benchmark for the lowest prices that are proving difficult for specialty retailers to compete with. This section outlines different pricing types and a suggested model for a competitive price structure.

Hi-Lo versus EDLP[97]

Hi-Lo pricing is where daily prices are generally higher but more frequent price promotions are offered at temporarily lower prices. Hi-Lo pricing can be used to improve your retail brand awareness and customer traffic to your store through promotional activity and is a powerful tool to increase sales turnover and cash flows. However, Hi-Lo pricing can erode consumer confidence in everyday shelf prices and so affect sales volume.

Every-day-low-pricing (EDLP) strategy sets lower average prices with smaller differences between the regular and promoted prices. The advantages of using EDLP are that it can restore price credibility with the consumer, it's simple and consistent and so is easier to communicate a lowest price image to consumers. However, it can significantly erode retailer profitability. Both pricing strategies have their distinct advantages and their distinct disadvantages.

The most relevant and effective pricing strategy for specialty retailers in today's information rich world where consumers have price checking at their fingertips, is that you are competitive using EDLP *only* where you need to be. It is your overall average margin that must be retained in order for you to maintain a profitable business.

In the past, retailers have often applied a blanket margin to the cost of all of their goods to come up with a selling price. This strategy is no longer applicable due to the price transparency that online and smart phone technologies provide the consumer. It's important to understand that you are often competing with global online sellers and not just the national big guys. Formalising your pricing structure will help you compete and maintain a profitable business.

Introducing the competitive pricing model

I have created a model that advocates for a diversified approach to retail pricing structure. It outlines classifying your stock into the categories of price sensitive lines, multiple margin lines, full margin lines and promotional lines. This process will help you define and manage an effective pricing structure that is balanced, flexible and incorporates Hi-Lo and EDLP strategies.

Products or price points that your competitors advertise in a catalogue or that can be seen online can be classified as *price sensitive lines*. These products are often national brands that have enjoyed mass media advertising and are established in your marketplace. You compete daily with these prices and market leaders most likely buy better than you. These items may also be stock that your competitors unfortunately, are dumping into your marketplace at unsustainable prices.

You may have bought these products from a supplier who has applied their margin on top of their landed cost price, further adding to your buy price. Often, product brands with the most equity or 'pull' are those that have the lowest margin. Pricing of these items needs to stay within a few dollars of your competitors or you risk being perceived as uncompetitive and irrelevant by today's savvy consumer.

Ask yourself if there is an alternative product or brand that makes you a better margin or is there a way you can shorten your supply chain in order to better compete on price sensitive items. When price sensitive items are price marked at RRP or above, you risk projecting the message that you are uncompetitive on every item in your store and that just may not be the case.

Multiple margin lines are products at low price points that you can add a 50, 100, 200 percent or higher margin to and still sell volumes. For example, a low priced generic branded paintbrush may cost you $2.50. You can easily sell it day-in and day-out for $15.00, in effect setting your own price and still competing with market leading offers.

The multiple margin applied in this case is 5 times or 500%! This is 83.33% profit on a low price point, so best placement for these lines is in high traffic area hotspot displays, like next to the counter in a dump bin and in the accessories section on a gondola end to ensure high volume of high margin sales.

Full margin lines are items that you price at RRP or in some cases, above RRP. Overall pricing decisions come back to what consumers will pay. This is known as 'what the market will bear'. Staples that are non-price sensitive are full margin lines. The margin gained when selling these lines often makes up for the lower margins applied to price sensitive lines and brings up your average margin to help sustain your RBM.

Market leaders often advertise a 'loss-leader' selling high volumes of product with no or little profit in order to get customers through the door. These are known as *promotional lines.* This strategy is used to entice those customers to buy multiple margin or full margin lines during the same visit to the store or to create or enhance customer loyalty.

Often the loss-leading product has been purchased from a supplier at a special price or has a rebate deal attached that supports the retailer's profit margin. You may not be able to afford to lose money on a promotional offer *but* be prepared to make a smaller margin on promotional lines for short periods of time. The trick is to maximise add-on sales at full or multiple margin during promotional periods. Placing them in hotspot locations is the best strategy. Here is a pie graph outlining an example of a diverse margin pricing approach. 58% of your stock is priced at full margin, 20% has multiple margin applied, 15% is promotional product and 7% is price sensitive. Each category and store may differ.

The competitive pricing model

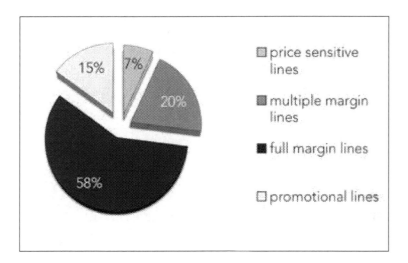

- □ price sensitive lines
- ■ multiple margin lines
- ■ full margin lines
- □ promotional lines

15% 7% 20% 58%

Paint shop under done

When Rach and Mishy 'put their BIG on' and price checked their competitors, they found they needed to make some price adjustments. On some national brands, they were asking too much. However, much to their surprise, many full margin lines were drastically under priced when compared closely. Rach and Mishy quickly repriced these items upwardly to meet market pricing and found they made up for the downward repricing of price sensitive items. Rach and Mishy continue to price check weekly to ensure their pricing structure remains competitive. **Price check your competitors regularly to revise pricing up or down**

Positioning of promotional lines

Whenever department stores have 30% off Bonds, I go and buy Bonds underwear. It's not often I buy Bonds unless it's reduced by 30% (Hi-Lo pricing). I buy volume when this offer is put forward and that's what large retailers count on. However, whenever I go to buy Bonds, I notice that the latest styles in brands such as Bendon, Berlei and Sass n Bide are positioned on racks next to the sale items at full price with full margin! It's very tempting to buy the new styles at full price! **During a sale event, place some full margin lines in hotspot positions around your promotional or 'loss-leader' lines**

Quick Tips to prepare your pricing plan

1. **Consider** that price competitiveness is now local, national and global
2. **Diversify** your margins to aid in competitiveness
3. **Classify** products and brands into price sensitive, multiple margin, full margin and promotional lines to incorporate a mixture of Hi-Lo and EDLP pricing strategies
4. **Measure** overall margin to determine profitability
5. **Price check** your competitors weekly

Secret 20-Pep-up your promotions

A 'sale' sign that remains on your front window for six months is not a promotion. Christmas decorations that stay up from year to year are not a promotion and products that have Easter sale tickets on them in September, you guessed it, *are not a promotion!* Successful promotions are well planned, executed and measured through a project management approach and integrated with your branding and marketing strategies.

Planning, execution and evaluation

Your planning process should include the following: Good co-ordination of media, buying the right amount of stock (demand forecasting), timely delivery of promotional stock, internal buy-in for the sale event by staff, personal selling requirements versus abilities, internal communication about the sale event and merchandising standards.[98]

An effective way to formalise your promotional planning of activities is through the creation of a promotional calendar detailing every store promotion throughout the year. The calendar clearly outlines the sale theme, promotional tools such as signage, point-of-sale-materials, ticketing, samples, tastings, giveaways, in-store trials, aromas, spruiking (selling with a microphone and speaker), interactive screens, guest endorsers or appearances and advertising mediums that add to the success of your promotion and the customers shopping experience during that promotion.

Your promotional calendar can be detailed to include individual sales budgets, pricing strategies, size and location of the sale area, positioning of displays, supplier involvement, duration and timeline for actions, delegation of tasks to necessary staff, ordering requirements and advertising timelines. The development of a promotions checklist that ties in with your calendar is an invaluable tool to ensure all boxes are ticked and your promotion goes ahead without a hitch even in your absence, if required.

All information that is necessary to run the promotion effectively and efficiently should be included in the calendar. Formalising your promotional calendar in this way allows you to minimise error when delegating tasks and enables management to share information freely with staff to ensure smooth execution of promotional events.

Measuring your promotion's performance is important because it gives you the ability to improve the outcomes for the next promotion and helps promotional planning and execution to evolve over time. Keeping the elements that worked well for you and improving those elements that didn't is a great way to move forward and grow.

Comparing sales data from previous promotions can help you gauge the success of your campaigns and feedback from customers and staff about what worked and what didn't is also a great way to measure your promotional performance. On the next page is a simple example of a promotional calendar:

2015 promotional calendar 'The deli delicious'

Timeline	Theme	Stock	Suppliers	Tools	Positioning	Pricing
2014 Dec 10-24	'Get ready for a Deli delicious Christmas with free home delivery on Xmas Eve!'	Puddings Prawns Hams Shortbreads Chocolates	Vision Australia GC Trawlers Wholesale meats Local producer 1 Local producer 2	Live Santa Claus In-store Posters Ticketing Lollie bags iPad home delivery service booking and ordering FB Email	Hotspot 1 Eye level cool cab Fridge display Front 2 aisle ends	Full price on all items this month Giveaway lollie bag to every customer
Dec 26-31	Post Xmas specials	Clearance Close to out of dates	No buying this month	Spruiker, Paul 10-12 and 4-5pm Sat Posters/ ticketing FB/ email	All hotspots around the store	20% off storewide clearance
Jan 1-15	Summer delights	Fresh salads	Made on site	Free small tub potato salad with every 500g salami FB/email	Centre of cabinet	Small tub $5 Medium $8 Large $10
Feb 1-10	Gelateria	Fresh gelati	Local producer 3	Tasting, giveaways FB/email	Promotional fridge at front of store	1 scoop $5 2 scoops $7 Tub $10
March 15-31	Chocolaterie	Chocolates	Lindt Local producer 4 Cadbury Schweppes	Tasting Interactive screen FB/email	Chocolate maker in the window	
April 10-20	Barra for easter	Fresh barramundi Prawns	GC Trawlers Australian caught	Fish promo posters/ tickets Large fish character at front FB/email	Centre cabinet	$25 kilo

Timeline	Theme	Stock	Suppliers	Tools	Positioning	Pricing
May 1-31	Bread for the soul	Organic sourdough Spelt mega grain Baguettes	Sol Organic farmers market Local bakery	PR campaign local paper ads Posters/ tickets FB/email	At counters Baskets on ends	Buy 2 baguettes for $10
June 1-15	Olive harvest	Green Black Sicilian Olive oil Olive soap	Barossa olives Hunter olives Penisi wholesalers Barossa fine foods	Tastings FB/email	Centre of cabinet	Premium olives Tub price $10 large
July 1-15	Winter vegetable fair	Carrots Potatoes Sweet potatoes Parsnips Leeks	Farmers market	Recipe ideas handouts		

It's no easy task to cut through the promotional 'noise' that consumers are bombarded with from retail stores on a daily basis. *Channel capacity* is the amount of messages consumers can take in at once from your store. Simple, concentrated, consistent and direct promotional messages coupled with repetition are the most effective way to cut through and deliver your message.

Eliminate any additional messages or non-promotional noise coming from extra posters, pictures or unnecessary clutter in or on windows, walls and above eye level. This will allow your promotion to be the focal point of your store and ensure that funds spent on advertising are tied-in with your store's merchandising.

Tying in P-O-P materials

Point-of-purchase (P-O-P) materials are posters, cardboard dump bins, competition entry forms, shelf talkers, shelf wobblers, floor graphics, catalogues, brochures and anything else that you can use to 'tie-in' your marketing and advertising dollar with your in-store presentation.

Positioning posters for promotions above hotspot displays and presenting highlighted merchandise to shoppers at the front of the store will help to tie-in your promotions. Position shelf-talkers and shelf-wobblers with shelf products to highlight promotional items and place competition pads at counters and in high traffic areas to improve the outcome of your promotions.

In some categories, consumers are up to 48 times more likely to make in-store buying decisions when P-O-P displays are present than when they are not, so displays have an incredible influence on consumer behaviour.[99] Despite this information, up to 50% of P-O-P materials supplied by manufacturers (to the grocery industry), are never used by retailers.[100]

Communication

Information to your customers about promotions needs to be regular, relevant and concise. Why not communicate to your customers the way that best suits their demographic? For example, Generation Y customers might like to find out about your event via SMS or through social media platforms such as FB and Twitter.

Many leading retail brands reach their targets through social media updates that are informative and engaging. Generation X customers may respond to glossy colour brochures or postcards sent via direct snail mail outlining sale details. Baby boomers may respond to a phone call inviting them personally to a store sale or to an email inviting them to a pre-sale or VIP event.

It is important to consider each customer segment and how you can enhance the effectiveness of your **communication** with your customers in order to cut through the daily noise to which they are exposed. *Imagine how we will communicate effectively with the next generation!*

Communicado boo boo

A new customer Johnathon, called me about stocking my wholesale product at his stall in a suburban weekend market. By his voice, I estimate that he would have been a baby boomer. The company policy was to supply retailers with a shop front only. My General Manager wanted a photo of Jonathon's stall before we made a decision about supply. I sent an SMS to Johnathon asking for a picture of his stall to be sent to my iPhone. That weekend he did so, and I forwarded it on to the GM on the following Monday via SMS. The decision was made not to supply him. Considering the last communication I had with him was through text message, I replied to Johnathon very politely via SMS and informed him that we would not be supplying him. The next day, I got a phone message from a very upset Jonathon telling me I was the rudest sales rep he had ever encountered and how dare I send him a text message rather than call him. He was extremely upset that I had not called him to break the news. His perception and my motivation were worlds apart. I should have understood that Johnathon's expectation was a phone call. I needed to stop and consider what would be the most effective communication method to use with him and not just assume that I should reply using the same method as the last communication. **Keep in touch with your customers however it suits them**

Quick Tips to pep-up your promotions

1. **Approach** your promotions from a project management perspective
2. **Create** a promotional calendar
3. **Include** social media in your communications
4. **Tie-in** your promotions with your stock and P-O-P materials
5. **Communicate** with target segments by the most appropriate method

Secret 21- Sum up your servicescape

The term **servicescape** implies that your standard of customer service fits into a competitive landscape, just like your brand positioning, and that there are other elements apart from customers and staff involved. Consider the customer's perspective of their interaction with a retailer from beginning to end and beyond. Break down the process of delivering reliable, efficient and effective customer service to every customer, every time. Ask yourself why you are improving your servicescape, what it will be, how to deliver it and what else is involved when planning improvements.

Quality control, training, motivation, self-serve technologies, service management and measurement systems are all impacting factors on the ability to deliver a brand's servicescape. Your servicescape is only as good as it is reliable. That is, you can measure its reliability with every single interaction with every single customer. It seems that everyone has an idea about what great customer service means. *There are thousands of books on the topic!* It really is the simplest thing in the world but the most difficult to get consistently right. In a nutshell, customers need to feel important, appreciated and welcome. That doesn't sound so hard, *does it?*

Your first impressions, personal service, self-service, add-on service, after sales service, extra service, *service, service, service,* are all under the microscope by every single customer, every single day with every single transaction, and so customer service can be seen as a variable that affects the overall perception of your brand experience.

Designing your servicescape to align with your core values, retail mix and your overall brand vision is the most contemporary way to approach customer service standards. How can you make your standard unique in your surrounding servicescape?

Think of your store as a ride at Movie World. Have you ever been on the Scooby Doo spooky coaster? Try designing your customer experience from beginning to end, every step of the way just like a theme park ride or Potato Head Beachclub in Seminyak, Bali. Take these models and apply them to your retail context, then develop your people to deliver your experience to every customer, every time.

Management

Stellar customer service is a culture. It's a culture that is bred through great leadership, regular training and effective communication. Market leading retailers develop their employees weekly, shaping customer service representatives to be the best they can be to deliver a reliable experience to the consumer. Empowering employees with the authority to turn customer complaints into lifetime loyalties is a powerful way to improve the reliability of your servicescape or customer service to your customers.

Empowering General Manager

Jürg is a former GM at a five star golf resort. In his restaurants he empowered staff to fix problems on-the-spot as soon as possible. He believes that unresolved complaints get bigger and cost more to fix later. 'Do whatever it takes' Jürg says. 'Give away a free meal or one nights accommodation if you have to. Who cares, it costs nothing to fix and what's important is that the customer will come back!' Jürg made a point of personally calling every customer to ensure they felt personal satisfaction with their complaint outcome and to ensure they were willing to return. No wonder he was so successful in business. **Strive to turn customer complaints into lifetime loyalties immediately!**

One of the things that can create a poor first impression for the in-store customer experience is anything that tells them off before they do it! You know what I mean? Have you ever seen signs that say 'Do not touch' or 'If you break you pay', that sort of thing? *Of course I want to touch what I am going to buy!* It's absurd that I would not be allowed to pick up, feel or try a product that I am going to invest my hard earned cash in. If I break something in your store, of course it was an accident!

In this era where experiential retailing is the new standard, enabling touch, feel, smell and taste, is key to building the brand and product experience. Imagine Apple not allowing you to touch an iPad or Nespresso not allowing you to taste their coffee! Zara not allowing you to try on their clothes! These brands have integrated the senses into their brand experience.

It's quite ridiculous when you think about it in those terms, but retailers still put up signs that scare their customers away and tell them off before they look at anything. Imagine buying a car without first driving it or handing over thousands for a USA Fender Stratocaster without playing it first! *Sheesh!* Trying before buying is what differentiates bricks and mortar retailers over online e-tailers and so provides the most important point-of-difference for specialty retailers.

I once saw a sign stuck on a hand dryer in a restroom that said *'Only one sheet of paper per use, this is supplied by the coffee shop not by the landlord, if this service is abused we will not be supplying paper to wash your hands'*. This message was not only unnecessary telling the customers about the feud between the landlord and tenant about who was supplying paper, but it left me feeling that I would never have coffee in a place where people were so mean. It costs nothing to be nice! Market leaders build uninhibited product experiences into their branding.

Aussie Woolies lead the way

I was grocery shopping in Woolworths the other day and I reached for the tonic water. Unfortunately, as I picked up the 4-pack, the packaging broke and 4 small bottles of fizzy tonic smashed loudly on the floor. It was like tonic springs in the middle of the aisle! Within seconds, a lovely man was there with a broom. His first question was 'Are you alright madam?' 'Yes' I replied, 'I'm afraid the cardboard packaging gave way'. 'Don't worry I've got it. Would you like another one?' he asked with a big smile 'Yes please, I would like four actually'. He loaded up my trolley and sent me on my way to finish my shopping as a loyal customer. I didn't feel for a second that I had to pay for the broken tonic. I'm sure the supplier would have replaced them to keep Woolworths happy anyway. **Accidents are a Cost Of Doing Business (COB) and opportunities to make loyal customers**

Measurement

How can you measure your customer service standard? Firstly, it's important to experience other customer standards that exist. Visiting market leaders who are known for excellent service standards is a great place to begin when looking for a benchmark for your brand. You can develop a checklist that outlines your servicescape in detail and then test run it in your store or many stores to see how you fare. Mystery shoppers can help you ascertain how your staff perform in your absence and can highlight areas for improvement.

Relationships

Your brand's servicescape is largely dependent upon your *people* delivering it. Investing in your people costs less than not investing in them when you consider the cost to induct and train new staff. Rebranding your customer service gives you an exciting opportunity to raise the bar and design a new dynamic model that enhances your positioning, core values, personality and overall brand equity.

Your people must first be aware of your customer service standard before they can perform to it and so, must be developed by your organisation to achieve that standard. If you are a small store with only one staff member, it is even more important that you spend time nurturing that relationship so you can develop trust to rely on one another daily in order to deliver your brand's service standard to every customer.

A formal induction process that welcomes new staff members to the organisation and shows them 'the ropes' is a great way to begin setting your new standard. A mentoring program where more experienced staff help to develop newcomers encourages personal development for both the mentor and the newcomer and subsequently impacts positively on your culture and service standard.

If you have young people working for you, it is important to understand that they may not be aware of your organisational expectations and so they need to be made aware of the benchmark you have set and coached to that standard. It doesn't matter if you have two staff members or two thousand, broadening your culture and developing those individuals will always serve to enhance your business and your life.

Training and personal development is an integrated and valued part of people investment for market leaders. They understand the power of developing loyal staff as human brand *touchpoints* that are capable of brand building with every customer interaction.[101]

Over the years, I have learnt that negative input achieves nothing with nobody and that focusing on positive feedback not only gets better results, it makes you feel better! In the words of Pema Chodron, the first American woman to become a Buddhist nun, 'One harsh word can undo a lifetime of kindness'.[102] People thrive on recognition and positivity and you can spend years developing great relationships that can be ruined in a moment of anger or mean spiritedness.

Recently, I had dinner with social media guru, Ted Rubin from New York. The philosophy outlined in his book 'Return on Relationship' (ROR)™ is to invest in relationships using social media as a primary vehicle. 'ROR is the value (both perceived and real) that will accrue over time through loyalty, recommendations and sharing, and is used to define and educate companies, brands, and people about the importance of creating authentic connection, interaction, and engagement'.[103] His mantra is improving relationships to improve business. *Simple!*

Contemporary approaches to management outline effective communication that enhances relationships and creates powerful team cultures that get results. Ask yourself how can you enhance the lives of your people and your customers through positive reinforcement and inputs that deliver outstanding returns on your relationships.

Some years ago I was the only sales rep in the company who achieved the budget for the quarter. I got a $500 bonus! *Yeah!* The thing that meant more to me than the bonus was the hand written note left on my desk from the CEO thanking me for my hard work and effort. Three months later I was promoted to state manager and awarded an industry commendation. His personal positive reinforcement spurred me on to work harder the next quarter and achieve and exceed the company budgets many times over. A small input from him resulted in a large output from me.

Saying goodbye to customers

Whilst visiting small retailers in rural Australia, I stayed at the Jones Hotel Group Comfort Inn, Wangaratta. I checked in and went to my room, ordered room service and went to sleep. Nothing unusual. After breakfast the next morning, I went to check out and Jilly on reception was spectacular! She processed two guests at the same time whilst keeping a third (me) happy to wait. She was friendly and efficient. I commented on her good job and went to my car. Arriving at my hire car, I noticed a small note under the wipers. It said *'Good morning, your windscreen has been cleaned with our compliments. Please drive safely today, we look forward to your return. Thank you for staying with us'.* Am I going back? *Hell yes!* It's the small things that make a massive difference.

When I was telling my story some days later by word-of-mouth, the retailer I was telling knew which hotel group I had stayed with and correctly named them. They are known in the region for their excellent service standard and staff development. I went back again some nine months later and got exactly the same service from Jilly! **The return on this relationship (ROR) is repeat business. How can you put a price on lifetime loyalty?**

Selling skills

I recently read that small retailers convert only 15% of customer foot traffic to sales. If this is a remotely accurate number, it is fair to say that there is room for improvement! If specialty retailers improved conversion rates to 30%, it would see sales figures double! IKEA have conversion rates from around 75%-95%, depending on economic and seasonal factors. That means most of their customers purchase something when visiting their stores, even if it is a $1 hotdog or a coffee in the cafeteria.

Imagine if you could double or even triple your figures without one new browsing customer! Stellar customer service and selling skills that improve sales conversion rates can impact dramatically on sales volume.

Customer service and selling are delivered at the same time but require very different skill sets to execute effectively. Customer service is looking after the customers needs and wants before, during and after their purchase. Selling skills are about guiding the customer through a sales process that leads to the purchase decision. Combining customer service design and delivery with a standard of formal *selling skills* will equip your staff with the knowledge they need to excel and improve sales conversion rates.

Not so clever Dick

I purchased a computer lead for $20 from a large electronics store to back up my work. I discovered when I got back to my office that I didn't need it after all. Then, some months later, I needed to buy ink cartridges for the office printer and so finally got around to taking it back. When I asked the guy for a refund, he said 'No, we can't do that.' I said 'Why not? I have the receipt and it's still in new packaging.' He said 'Why are you bringing it back?' I said 'Because I don't need it'. He said 'We have a 7 day returns policy and I can't take it back'. I said 'Are you sure you want to lose $500 a year in printer cartridge business?' He said 'I can't refund it.' I said 'Fine, I'll go somewhere else'. That said, I left $120 worth of ink on the counter and walked out! I now buy my cartridges online and get them cheaper. The guy should have at least offered me a store credit or given me a $20 discount on the cartridges to keep my long term business. Management needed to empower the assistant to make good decisions for the future of the business. **Empower your staff to make the right decisions to satisfy your customers**

Here's a simplified version of *Sell Products and Services* (SIRXSL001A), that you can share with your staff. It is an easy summary of a two day training unit from Certificate II in Retail, which is a national standard outlined by the Australian Government and delivered by registered training organisations (RTO) throughout Australia.

What to do	How to do it
1. Please	Create a positive first impression
2. Welcome	Greet, smile, make eye contact, build rapport
3. Inform	Share Product knowledge, features and benefits
4. Enable	Overcome objections
5. Ask	Open questions
6. Direct	Sell with confidence
7. Spoil	With customer service, add-on, after sales
8. Thank	Smile and be grateful
9. Farewell	Say goodbye
10. Invite	Come back again
CULTURE	*RESPECT CULTURAL DIFFERENCES*

This section explains the very simple steps to retail selling. I have remodeled the course to represent the customer's point of view to help you better understand the 10 steps in the buying and selling process. *Easy!*

As a customer, I want you to *please me.* That means my first impression of you is incredibly important and must be positive. How you look and if you smile at me will say everything I need to know immediately. If I don't like what I see, I may walk straight out of your store leading to a lost sale. I only get a first impression of you once, so it's important that you don't ignore me or overlook me and equally, don't smother me as soon as I walk into your store.

I want you to *welcome me* by looking me in the eye to make me feel important and appreciated with a nice greeting that is appropriate to building rapport. I don't want you to say 'Can I help you?' as I am automatically programmed to say 'No, I am just looking, thanks' and our relationship may end right there. I would much rather you said 'What brings you into [store brand] today?'

or 'Hi, welcome to our store, what can I show you that you might like?' I may browse for a while and then I may ask you a question.

Here's where I need you to *enable me* into my buying process. That is, help me understand what my needs and wants are and overcome any reasons or objections I have for not buying today. You may have to convince me subtly that I need what you are offering. To do this you can *ask me* open questions that require an answer longer than 'Yes' or 'No' that help me talk to you more about my needs and wants.

These are questions that get me thinking I might want to buy from you because you are helping me find what I need. Questions like 'Do you have a colour preference?' or 'Do you have an idea of the style you like?' I want you to *direct me* confidently by asking appropriate questions including if I want to buy, when I want to buy or how I want to pay. I don't want you to be pushy, insincere or aloof.

Once I have indicated that I am ready to buy through my body language or by saying 'Yes, I like this one', I want you to *spoil me* with outstanding service, add-on sales and after sales service. When I have handed over my hard earned cash and you have given me my goods, I want you to *thank me* for shopping with you and *farewell me* from your store inviting me to return in a friendly manner.

In the United States, some salespeople come out from behind the counter and hand the customer their bag of goods using both hands to part with it. In the Paul Smith store in the Las Vegas City Center, I once experienced the sales assistant walking me to the door and waving goodbye after making a very small purchase.

This is a very nice finishing touch that left me feeling confident that I made the right brand and product investment. Consumers often experience a feeling known as 'post-decision dissonance' or 'buyers remorse' where they doubt their buying decisions.[104] In my view, sales people who reinforce consumers with confidence that they have made a great choice, add to overall customer satisfaction and loyalty.

It is important and relevant to note that some Asian cultures have dos and don'ts when handling transactions. For example, when giving out business cards, returning credit cards or change to people from Indonesia and China, it's best to use both hands as a subtle yet meaningful way of showing respect and awareness of their culture. Malaysians and Indians consider the left hand unclean and so it is preferred to use only the right hand for all transactions.[105]

Pointing with your index finger is considered rude in many Asian cultures and so using the thumb is the best way to point out items or point to directions. No matter which culture your customer is from, it is polite to respect and deliver their expectations and incorporating these small touches into your steps to selling will build customer brand loyalty.

Asleep!

In an International airport recently, I noticed an employee sprawled out on a desk at the front of the store in full view of passersby. She was sound asleep and she was definitely not wearing a nametag! Very difficult to deliver stellar customer service when one is asleep! **What would your first impression of that be?**

Applescape

I recently went into a suburban Apple store for an iPhone 4 screen protector (I know it's an old model). It was Friday morning around 11.00am and the store had around 60 people in it. My immediate thought was that I might have to wait for customer service. I continued to the accessories section of the store and was happy with the prices (noting that the price had been reduced by half which better reflects global competitiveness). I took the screen protector off the fixture and held it in front of me as I looked at it. Immediately, Tim, wearing his nametag said to me 'Did you just want the protector or did you need something else?' I replied, 'No, just this thanks'. He said 'Go down the front to Fiona on the door and she will put it through for you. I said 'Okay, thanks Tim'. I walked down the front to find Fiona (also wearing a nametag) through the crowded rear of the store. Immediately she said 'Can I put this on for you?' I said 'Yes please' she said 'Are you paying by card?' I said 'Yes'. Fiona pulled out her iPod touch equipped with a card reader and swiped my card for payment. 'Can I have your email address please and I will send you a receipt right away'. I gave it to her and I was out of that shop in less than 7 minutes. On the bottom of the emailed receipt was an invitation to give feedback in the form of a survey. It took 2 minutes, so I did it! What a treat and what a great model for innovative and sustainable retailing. Apple also now has my email address on their database and regularly send me product updates and marketing communication. **Can you incorporate something from this into your own RBM?**

Do I know you?

In a LuLuLemon store on a Sunday morning after a leisurely breakfast with Sal, Meges and Rosita, we ogled over beautiful products in a beautifully presented store. There was a woman standing on a step near the counter folding clothing. When I looked at her, she caught my eye and said 'Hi' to me like she was a long lost friend. She engaged with me on a very personal and open level to the point where I thought I already knew her. After saying 'Hi' back, she told me briefly and succinctly that the store alters any clothing purchases free of charge. I didn't even realise, but in less than 5 seconds, she had connected and transferred the information to me effortlessly and my value perception of the brand increased. I was really just looking and had not planned to make a purchase but because of my interaction in this delightful way, I ended up buying 2 pairs of socks @ $20 each. **Engage with customers in a relaxed and friendly manner**

Snobby shop girl

Friends were over for lunch and started talking about Oprah Winfrey experiencing racism in a handbag store in Europe where the shop assistant miraculously did not recognise the most famous face in the world! Apparently, when Oprah asked to look at a handbag that was highly priced the shop assistant replied 'Oh, no it's too expensive.' Oprah and her pots of money left the store empty handed immediately. It's the typical pretty woman scenario where sales people judge customers by what they are wearing or by the colour of their skin. **It's important to ensure this type of retail snobbery does not exist on any level in your servicescape**

Real estatescape

Barbara was a real estate agent for the Professionals. One day there was a fellow, Roger, in muddy clothing, unshaven and in her words 'wet and filthy', looking at the listings in the office window. No one in the office would go outside to speak to him based on his appearance. Barbara took the initiative and went outside in the rain to chat with the stranger and ended up marrying him. First she sold him a $1m home! **Barb always says never judge a book by its cover!**

Jeweller too good

Over Easter 2013, we had a family wedding. Our bride and English groom were on holiday from the UK and feeling relaxed in their casual beach clothes as they organised their big day. The couple went into a boutique jewellery store on the Gold Coast to look at wedding bands. The jeweller intimated that the exclusive jewelry would be too expensive for the couple and that they were wasting each other's time. Needless to say our couple promptly left and spent $1000 with Michael Hill who delivered excellent customer service and outstanding customer satisfaction. **The customer is always right!** Harry Gordon Selfridge, Selfridge & Co.

Quick Tips to sum up your servicescape

1. **Create** your own brand **servicescape** experience
2. **Empower,** communicate and develop your staff to implement the standard to every customer, every day, every time
3. **Develop** knowledge and practice the 10 simple steps to selling
4. **Reward** performance with praise and positive reinforcement
5. **Avoid** retail snobbery at all costs
6. **Never** judge customers by how they look
7. **Remember** the customer is always right

The elements we have covered in rebranding redesign are location, layout, store design, merchandise assortment, visual merchandising, pricing, promotions and customer service. All of these together make up the largest part of your rebranding program. By applying innovation and sustainability to every part of your RBM and retail mix and incorporating an online segment to your business, you can be assured that you will succeed into the future!

To let you in on as many secrets as possible, here is an example of a 'pilot' rebranding program undertaken in Australia in December 2013. The Retail Food Group's 'Project Evolution'[106] has seen updates to the 'Brumby's Bakery' brand in 11 of the 27 secrets in **Retail Rebranded.** These updates can be applied to any retailer. They include:

1. Secret 4-Incorporate sustainability: A new organic colour palette of browns and timber finishes has been unveiled by the brand's pilot store sending a message of a move toward more sustainable retailing.
2. Secret 5-Innovate: The retailer has incorporated digital screens showing menu offers.

3. Secret 6-Go online: The retailer is reported to have incorporated an e-commerce component to its RBM.

4. Secret 8: Get a Brand personality: A refreshed new logo and packaging 'builds a bridge' from the old personality to the new and retains brand equity by making subtle incremental change that consumers can recognise as legitimate.

5. Secret 11: Position your brand clearly: The retailer has rebranded to position it's brand as a market leader.

6. Secret 14: Choose the right location: New stores are located outside traditional shopping centres in convenient locations.

7. Secret 16: *Sass up* your store design: The retailer has incorporated an updated contemporary new look for the brand.

8. Secret 17: Modify your merchandise assortment: A wider range of product is now offered including espresso coffee.

9. Secret 19: Prepare a pricing plan: The value for sale has been lifted (higher pricing).

10. Secret 23-Include social media: Social media is now a focus to get in touch with Brumby's new customer segments.

11. Secret 24-Audit your brand touchpoints: New signage has been installed and staff have been kitted out with new uniforms. Note that not all brand touchpoints have been updated and these will need to be audited nationally if the pilot is rolled out.

Note that Brumby's also updated *Secret 15-Maximise your layout.* However, in my view, the change to store layout incorporating a walk-in style does not allow customers to self-serve and therefore will not maximise potential of sales volume whilst minimising staffing costs. Finally, here's a summary flow chart that outlines the key areas that make up rebranding redesign. This model can be applied to your rebrand now, whoever you are and wherever you are!

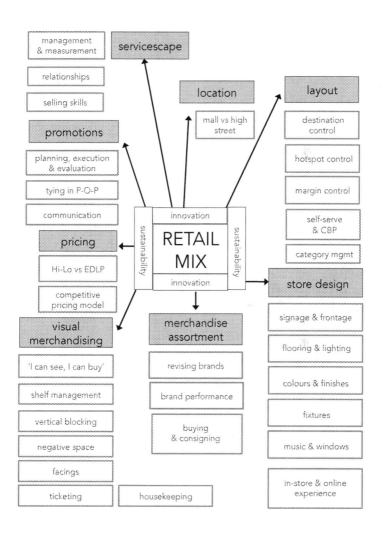

Adapted from Dale Miller. *Retail Marketing. A Branding and Innovation Approach.* Tilde University Press, 2008.

5- relaunch

Secret 22-Remodel your marketing communications

The most effective approach to marketing communications is an integrated one. The elements of the marketing communications process include 'advertising, sales promotions, personal selling, product packaging, point-of-purchase materials, billboards, public relations and sponsorships'.[107] Sending a consistent message through these channels is important to build brand equity.

Communicating your revised brand meaning to your new customer segments without alienating your existing customer base is vital for building new customer connections and relationships.[108] For example, a new customer segment may be your Facebook (FB) website 'friends', perhaps a younger demographic that you have never before communicated with.

How do these customers differ from your existing in-store loyal purchasers and what are their expectations of communications from your brand? *'Put your BIG on'* and observe the FB websites of leading retailers to see what content is delivered. 'Like' pages and posts (comments) and become friends so you can see what's going on in the hearts and minds of the consumers of your competitors.

Learn what *not* to do by observing comments on social networking sites (SNS) and how to handle negative word-of-mouth incidents by observing how market leaders respond on their social media platforms. What sort of promotional messages do market leaders post? What are the responses from the new segment? Build your FB website, Twitter, Instagram, Pinterest and other accounts with that in mind and make posts according to how the segment communicates with each other.

Use your youngest and brightest resources to help you create and maintain your SNS. Ask your kids to help out for some pocket money. You'll find your 'Likes' will improve and traffic to your website will increase. Imagine building these tasks into a job description: 'Full time shop assistant required, must be conversant with social media' LOL! Gen Y's are all conversant and they love to be part of your brand transformation.

Market leading retail brands hire full-time staff to update and maintain their SNS in order to connect with new segments, so building this type of task into a sales assistant role will save you money and keep your staff happy at the same time. Who cares if staff spend 30 minutes a day looking on their own FB website as long as they get your brand's 'Likes' up and share your posts with their friends, increasing your brand awareness and reach.

Tell your customers about your rebrand through every possible communication channel you have available to you including those elements of advertising, sales promotions, personal selling, product packaging, point-of-purchase materials, billboards, public relations and sponsorships. If you don't communicate what you are doing, how will your target markets know who you are and what you do?

Secret 23-Include social media

It is possible you cannot afford to incorporate advertising, point-of-purchase materials, billboards, public relations and sponsorships into your marketing communications. Using **social media** to communicate with target markets is a given for retailers of today and it allows you opportunity to communicate with your customers daily through a channel that is contemporary, low cost, competitive and relevant to a growing segment of today's consumers.

Social media is the very best way to compete with market leaders. Consider using social media in conjunction with your database to send out information that is presented in a relevant way and has the capability to access thousands of people. Let's say you post a special or a new product arrival on your FB site. Your store has 1000 friends. If only 100 of those friends like your post it could be exposed to thousands of others of their friends. FB users now total 1.15 billion worldwide and the average user has 130 friends.

Harry Selfridge, owner of the first department store in London, was a visionary. With the arrival of television he stated 'Television is not going away'. He was right! Imagine a world without television? The Internet and social media are not going away either. Social networking sites are here to stay. Experts say that 'online advertising is superior to traditional media because it provides consumers with virtually full control over the commercial information they choose to receive, or to avoid' and that the Internet is a key element of marketing communications.[109] The fact remains that there are no market leading retailers in the world prepared to ignore the power of social media!

Better than the phone

Sam, a Gen-Y owns a restaurant. He posted a function invitation to his FB friends. Within 5 days he had secured 45 ticket sales and booked out his small restaurant without picking up a phone or printing off a flyer! Sam had the security of knowing his restaurant will be full before he orders for catering and before his staff began preparation. The cost to promote this event was zilch! Sam connected with his regulars and friends via social media on a marketing budget of zero! **Social media is a powerful marketing tool**

Secret 24-Audit your brand touchpoints

Any product, service, transaction, venue, or experience through which your customers receive a significant impression of your brand is a point that your customers connect with known as a brand 'touchpoint'. They can be interpreted as all of the physical, communication and human interactions that customers and stakeholders experience with your retail brand.[110]

Brand touchpoints can be explained in three distinct segments of pre-purchase, purchase and post-purchase. Pre-purchase touchpoints include your public relations, online presence, advertising and the collection of media used to support sales such as letterheads, business cards, flyers and printed materials known as 'marketing collateral'. Purchase touchpoints are your product and service assortment, point-of-purchase (POP) materials, displays and personal selling. Lastly, *post-purchase* brand touchpoints are your servicescape, billing, loyalty programs, product quality and newsletters.[111]

The rebranding goal is to identify all touchpoint opportunities and send the same integrated message about your brand using them as your vehicle. It's not as easy as it sounds when one of the challenges retailers face today is that not all touchpoint communication channels such as social media, for example, can be controlled.

Social networking and bloggers take the reins out of the hands of retailers and marketers and into the hands of consumers. The tactic now used by market leaders is to 'use social media to listen to their customers, offer services to engage, interact through forums to enhance the brand experience, recommend based on behaviour to drive personal transactions and support and reward customers post-sale to keep them coming back'.[112] The best overall strategy is to develop an integrated multi-touchpoint approach that supports your brand experience and builds customer loyalty.

I once received a Virgin Australia silver Velocity membership package in my post office box. *OMG!* It was beautifully presented in matte silver packaging with a personalised welcome letter and luggage tags enclosed. I felt so privileged to be a lounge member, that I was hooked for life! The loyalty program and lounge membership is a touchpoint for the Virgin brand and it succeeded in building my unwavering brand loyalty. Now as a gold member, I only fly Virgin where possible.

I love the brand and since the recent rebranding program saw updates to the name, logo, signage, staff uniforms, lounge, luggage tags and service protocols, I have observed that it's much harder to get a seat in the lounge than it used to be! In fact, my local airport has already outgrown its lounge capacity and opened a mini-lounge for the busy times to minimise customer wait times and avoid overcrowding, further enhancing the *consumer flying process!*

Today's consumer expects no less than a brand experience and that experience is enabled through brand touchpoints. International market leaders Starbucks, Zara, Nespresso, IKEA and Apple all have their own brand personality and brand promise accompanied by a brand experience and touchpoints that are consistent with their brand meanings. Conduct an audit on your touchpoints to see if you have a strong and integrated marketing message.

Touchpoint breakdown

Brand **touchpoint breakdowns** occur all the time, all over the place, even to global brands. Many brands experience a 'disconnect' with some of their touchpoints such as out-of-date logos, fading signage, dated shop fittings and poor customer service. I'm sure you can think of brands that fit this description. These elements reflect the positioning of those brands with declining market share and negative attitudes that consumers express toward them as they head toward irrelevance in today's competitive brandscape.

Conducting a touchpoint audit on your brand can expose breakdowns that can be improved and 'plugged'. The most common specialty retail touchpoint breakdown is a logo, colour or font on a staff uniform, sticker or sign that has not yet been updated.

These touchpoint breakdowns can be easily fixed once you become aware of them. It is important to assess the cost of updating brand touchpoints when you embark on the rebranding journey, as some can be updated quickly and at low cost and others can be quite expensive to change and so get left behind or given low priority.

In summary, the most important strategy is to offer a one-brand experience everywhere. Contemporary advice for the best retail touchpoint strategy suggests the path forward is to 1) identify your core target shoppers, 2) understand how they interact with media, today and in the future, 3) develop an integrated multi-touchpoint strategy that fits the brand and matches shopper behavior, 4) listen to consumers voices in these touchpoints and, 5) respond appropriately.[113]

Secret 25- Create brand buy-in

Consider your personnel as human brand touchpoints who need to **buy-in** to your rebrand in order for you to succeed. They can believe in your brand and even love it! This is known as a brand 'lovemark'.[114] They can actually become empowered retail brand touchpoints.

The 'Cheesecake Factory' in America develops their brand ambassadors (staff) by holding daily meetings, quizzing them on menus and cheesecake culture and training and rewarding staff for their brand enthusiasm. The benefits of this program are ultimately transferred to the consumer. Part of the chain's multi-billion dollar success and year on year growth is attributed to its brand engagement program.[115]

The Cheesecake Factory brand experience is one I still talk about, some five years after experiencing an outstanding and competitive food and wine menu, enthusiastic customer service, an enjoyable environment and a new perspective on global standards in the restaurant business, not to mention the *cheesecake!*

Your brand ambassadors can understand, embrace and educate others about what your brand stands for. One way to promote this kind of 'buy-in' from your staff is to fit your staff demographic to your brand and your offer. Think of Virgin Australia as an example. Virgin staff all buy-in to the Virgin experience of their customers. They are adaptable, friendly and loyal to their brand.

Popular Aussie fashion retailer 'Cotton On', whose target segment is under 25s fit their staff demographic to their brand that showcases walking staff touchpoints in every store. Apple ambassadors are all crazy about their employer brand and wear their exclusive blue Apple t-shirts with a sense of brand belonging and proud representation.

You may need to change attitudes about the old brand to the new brand. Although it may seem difficult sometimes, it is vital to overcome internal resistance to change in order to gain full support for your branding updates. Devising a plan to achieve this through training and buy-in is the best way.

Internal buy-in is essential for successful retail rebranding and provides a solid platform for *external* stakeholder buy-in. Associations, partners, investors, suppliers and customers all need to buy-in to your revised brand in order for your rebranding to be successful.

Specialty retailers can rarely afford mass media advertising to change old attitudes. Sustainable, cheap and effective ways to relaunch your new brand such as public relations (PR), media interviews, editorial in the local paper and social media that directly involves your customers, will all aid your rebranding buy-in participation.

Developing brand ambassadors who spread the word and engage with social media on your brand's behalf are valuable assets so be sure to communicate your new brand benefits to your existing and new customer segments through all your available touchpoint channels.

Brand ambassador

Do you have a check out guy or girl at your local supermarket that you have been chatting to for years? Steve has been serving me at the checkout for almost 12 years, until self-serve checkouts made my dealings with him less frequent! When I asked Steve what he liked about working for his organisation he replied, 'It's the personal development and training they have given me and the safe and professional working environment that I like the most'. **Personal development is highly valued by employees**

Secret 26-Develop your people

In my view, professional development is actually personal development. If you help your people develop as individuals through awareness and knowledge, it will benefit them, you *and* your business. Invariably you will have some star performers on the payroll and probably some underperformers. As I mentioned, incorporating a mentoring program in which your stars take the underperformers under their wing and help mentor them to a higher standard works well.

This approach helps share the knowledge surrounding the business, which improves your economic sustainability and your stress levels! It also gives your performers a pat on the back and helps younger or newer staff with their confidence levels so that personal relationships flourish and social sustainability improves.

As individual abilities improve, be sure to recognise the improvements and listen to feedback. Social functions can help to build a strong team and provide an environment where team members can express their thoughts more freely. Sometimes a simple cup of coffee as a reward for outstanding service to your brand is enough to keep staff feeling confident and positive about their working conditions. Happy and valued employees are more likely to buy-in to your rebrand and so become walking brand ambassadors.

Ask your staff what they like and dislike about their workplace through an anonymous questionnaire. Place a suggestion box in the lunchroom and encourage communication about new ideas that improve working conditions. Ask them how they can make your store a better place for customers to shop and allow them input into your rebranding program. Listen to their suggestions and they will feel valued.

It's important to include young minds as they are a valuable resource and often carry up-to-date innovative ideas that can transform your business. Before you know it, you will be known as the best place to work and your quality of staff and retention rate will improve.

Internal changes lie with you. Great leaders build great brands. Think Richard Branson and Steve Jobs! You are the leader and so it is entirely up to you what sort of internal culture you breed for your brand. As the head of your organisation, taking an educational approach to develop your people can be an inspirational way to lead rebranding change. Your role is to energise and mobilise your people. Get them thinking about what they are doing and how they can contribute to your brand.

Empowering your people to be able to think for themselves and make daily decisions within their abilities and roles is good management that makes people accountable for their choices. Of course, developing yourself as a leader and manager will allow you to pass on those skills to your people and relieve you from micro managing daily operations. Reading books, taking online courses and further education can improve your own awareness as to what style of management you would like to incorporate into your RBM.

A strategy adopted by the top two US market leaders, Walmart and Home Depot is to reinvest 5c out of every $1 of profit back into the business to make staff development a reality. These retailers successfully use this model to fund their ongoing people development. If it works for these market leaders, why can't it work for you?

The leadership circle of change outlines the process to undertake when incorporating organisational change.[116] By applying Dr. Bernice McCarthy's 4MAT learning system of 'Why, what, how, what if and what else?'[117] to the circle, you have a good starting point to plan your people management.

Communicate to your people *why* you are changing, *what* you are changing, *how* it is changing and outline *what if* and *what else* is relevant throughout change. This will ensure that you cover all aspects through a change management approach.

Leadership circle of change

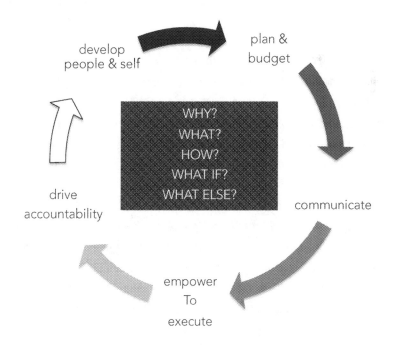

Secret 27-Look ahead

Customer shopping habits have changed forever and will forever change along with technological advances. The Internet is not leaving us anytime soon and shopping online will continue to grow. Best practice in retail will continue to evolve as retailers incorporate new and exciting ideas and continue to set the benchmark higher in order to offer a point of difference from online shopping and lure customers back into their stores.

I wonder what the smart phone of 2020 will look like? I wonder what short cuts it will provide and how much it will enhance the lives of people worldwide? Will consumers buy from holographic greeters in virtual change rooms and co-create or personalise their merchandise choices? Will they order from glass screens embedded in fridges and dining room tables? The technology is already available.[118]

You too can develop your business sustainability by opening your mind to change. Sending a clear message, altering your store to suit consumer behaviour, retaining the best staff, providing an easy, convenient and pleasant experience for consumers to buy from you and innovating will allow you to keep up with new directions.

Sustainability, innovation and experiential retailing are the new hallmarks of market leaders. Specialty retailers must follow in order to survive and grow into specialised market niche positions. Retail brands will evolve in line with consumers driving demand. Social media and word-of-mouth combined will demonstrate it can make or break retail, product and service brands.

Retailers who do not take an omni-channel revenue approach will decline in numbers and eventually fail. In-store retail will differ only through the *experiences* that retailers offer the consumer. Consumers will demand omni-channel purchasing and higher levels of interactivity anytime, anywhere, 24/7.

Large retailers will expand further into developing economies such as China and India to achieve growth as more people in those countries move into the middle class giving them more resources to lead markets and innovations. Supply chains will continue to shorten. As Australia's Asian population climbs above 2 million into the Asian century,[119] shopping centres that are relevant to new generations will become the centre of communities as they are in many Asian countries.

Sustainability and innovation will be integrated into building designs and materials as a new minimum standard evolves through neccessity.[120] Shopping clusters or concentrations of shops will intensify as demand for convenience and local food supply increases.[121] The high street renaissance with newly renovated shops will continue to enhance cluster opportunities for specialty retailers. Individually owned stores will find it harder to compete and specialty buying groups and franchises will grow as they offer competitive supply chains, pricing, marketing and promotions to small retailers.

Communities will begin to better understand sustainability and self-sufficiency concepts and the trend for community markets where people sell or swap for home-grown produce will continue rising. Coastal shopping precincts will diminish as the effects of global warming take place and coastal area living is redefined.[122]

This is where store location will be more important than ever. Do you have a plan for these changes into the future?

Quick Tips to step 5 relaunch

1. **Communicate** your rebrand to existing customers and new market segments
2. **Incorporate** social media platforms into your communication strategies
3. **Audit** your brand touchpoints to expose any breakdowns
4. **Create** a culture that encourages brand buy-in
5. **Develop** yourself and your people
6. **Continue** to innovate over time
7. **Plan** and prepare for the future

If you have made it to the end of this book, you are on the way to willing and active reinvention. Even if you take a small amount of this information and use it to improve your retail business model, my goal of helping you and countless retailers around the world raise the bar for the consumer experience has been achieved.

You may not be able to implement everything that is suggested throughout the rebranding journey and *that's okay!* My intention is for you to think about using some strategies in your own context based on your own experience to guide you through the rebranding process.

I hope **Retail Rebranded** lights a fire in your belly and inspires you to take on the challenges of today's retailscape so you can evolve into a relevant, innovative and sustainable brand flourishing in the global economy in which you now operate.

6-mall kiosk rebranding

The steps from **Retail Rebranded** are simplified in this section to suit **mall kiosk** or **Casual Mall Lease (CML)** retailers. As a kiosk retailer, you are most likely not a destination store, rather a diversion en route to a destination or 'anchor' retailer. Understand that you are selling impulse items and so your biggest draw card is the first impression you make on consumers that will entice them to stop and buy.

The mall kiosk mix

Store design and *visual merchandising* are the primary elements from the retail mix that enhance your first impression and make the biggest impact on consumers.

Once potential customers have stopped at your kiosk, your *merchandise assortment, perceived value pricing, customer service* and *housekeeping* will help ensure you capture your share of the market in your centre or mall. In order to improve your business towards growth, these are the key areas that require the most focus and therefore represent what I call the **mall kiosk mix**. For best results, mall kiosk retailers need to connect with passersby in every one of these eight retail mix elements.

1. Store design

Ensure that you display your retail brand name using quality *signage* that is featured with lighting, is tasteful and is meaningful to your customers. Meaningful signage outlines a relevant brand that is up-to-date and contemporary. Sometimes it might work best to call yourself by a descriptive name that tells consumers about your offer. Examples might be 'Jazzie Jewels' or 'Kids Korner', 'Sox n Jox' or 'Dress to Impress.' These names send a clear message to your customers about *who you are* and *what you do.*

Trestle tables have been outlawed from retail shopping malls for years and rightly so! *Nothing and I mean nothing, looks good on trestle tables!* High quality infrastructure will ensure high quality merchandising translating to a positive and impactful first impression to impulse shoppers.

It's difficult to make a general statement about which *fixtures* are the right ones to use. A mixture of cabinets, slat wall and risers will add interest and depth to your displays and together should tell a story about your retail brand. Avoid using unsightly or visibly worn infrastructure. Low cost recycled alternatives can add a contemporary element to your kiosk that also decreases your carbon footprint and sends a message of sustainability.

Using fixtures that are contemporary and appropriate for your stock will give best results and will showcase your merchandise in its best light. It's a great idea to open up thoroughfares so passing foot traffic is invited into your kiosk allowing customers to walk freely between fixtures. Face or point displays directly at oncoming foot traffic so consumers are more likely to stop and browse your kiosk.

Lights are very important to help highlight key stock items and should be aimed at merchandise and signage to showcase the most attractive features in the most attractive way. One well-lit feature display is enough to create a 'wow factor' that helps stop consumers in their tracks to browse your kiosk brand. Be brave and express your brand personality through the use of these elements of **store design** in your mall kiosk. *Go for it!*

2. Visual merchandising

There are a number of *display types* you can incorporate into your mall kiosk. Often, products arranged by *colour* and *vertical blocking techniques* rather than by product category and horizontal blocking will improve your overall attractiveness and first impression. This means that *all* of your stock belonging to a particular colour group is displayed together in vertical rectangles.

For example, if you sell handbags, accessories and jewellery, it is visually effective to place all red of these products on one fixture together. This can sometimes pose difficulties with fixtures that are not well designed for your stock so it is important when designing, buying or hiring fixtures that you consider this merchandising strategy.

The key is to place colour categories so that colours adjacent to each other align with today's fashion. For example, avoid placing an aqua blocked section next to an orange blocked section unless market leading fashion retailers are currently showcasing those colours together in their stores. It may be better to place aqua next to brown and red next to beige.

Australian market leader in fashion stationery 'Smiggle,' colour blocks fixtures throughout stores to achieve effective consumer stopping power! Shoppers find this approach to clean lines, minimal clutter and space around items especially pleasing to the eye in a shopping mall environment, and are more likely to stop and browse.

Observe what your competitors do by visiting their stores (benchmarking) and make changes to your store that appear to work for them. Black or white colour blocks can be used as a buffer between potentially clashing colours. Colour blocking is an excellent strategy to incorporate into your kiosk, so don't be afraid to implement these techniques as soon as you can!

Here is a diagram that simplifies how to build displays that sell through the implementation of colour and vertical blocking techniques. Note the lights above displays to highlight merchandise.

Colour blocking kiosk displays

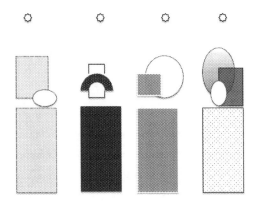

3. Merchandise assortment

Your shopping centre marketing or leasing manager will be able to give you a description of the customer segments that visit your centre or mall. This is called your customer 'demographic' and is valuable information when you are deciding which products to buy for resale. Make sure you purchase with your customers' needs and tastes in mind. After all, you don't want to have a store full of products that visitors to your mall and kiosk don't want to buy.

Stocking products across low, medium and high price points allows you to appeal to a wider customer demographic and creates an interesting shopping environment. Individual pieces can be merchandised to show consumers what makes you unique and different to other retailers in your mall. Be sure to position your feature display so all foot traffic can see it.

Incorporating items that have a mid-range price point that essentially become your bread and butter lines is a good idea to create interest in your *merchandise assortment*. Including lower priced items that sell in high volumes are helpful for daily cash flow, as often consumers will pay cash for those items. Additionally, high priced items can often show off your distinctiveness from your competitors and enhance your profitability.

Barriers to buying

Whilst incorporating a higher merchandising standard for a women's fashion kiosk, I discovered that the owner was accessing direct supply from Indian fashion designers. His clothes were very high quality but there were a few barriers to buying. Together, we concluded that whilst Indian women are happy to show their arms in the hot Indian climate, Australian women are not so fussed and prefer medium length sleeves as they move into middle age. 99% of his stock was sleeveless! Whilst the kaftan style of dresses he stocked in a number of colours were popular to try on, the inside slips were proving too small for the average Australian woman. A number of other items were proving too short in the torso and so sales were poor as objections about style and fit were a major barrier to buying. **Buy or alter your stock with your target customers needs in mind**

4. Perceived value pricing

Pricing and price marking is critical in an impulse-buy situation. Generally, but not always, kiosk vendors sell on low price. That is totally fine, except the goods must look as though they are worth more than what you have marked them at. For example, if you price mark your products at $10 and you display them so they look like they are worth $20, you send a message of *high perceived value.*

Customers see good value in your offer and are happy to pay $10, feeling like they have snapped up a bargain. If, on the other hand, you display your $10 stock as if it's worth $5, you will project a messy, cluttered look and feel that makes your customers think your stock is priced too high. This is termed *low value perception.* Customers will dismiss your offer and may not even stop to browse, based on their first impression of the perceived value of your stock.

Make sure you have your best price marked on items upfront. Inflating the price and then selling at a lower price is not considered best practice in today's contemporary shopping mall environment. Mall shoppers do not expect to barter on price, so all stock must be ticketed in order for self-service to take place, which is essential for mall kiosk retailers who may only have one staff member at all times.

Price tickets must, along with brand signage, be of high quality and should be the same size or uniform throughout your stand. This will help to minimise clutter and maximise the perceived value of your goods on offer. Hand written posters or tickets should be avoided if possible.

Many kiosk retailers buy direct from overseas suppliers adding to economic sustainability through lower costs, higher margins and shorter supply chains. This is a good strategy in the scheme of things. However, many of the products that are purchased offshore from countries such as China, India, Malaysia and Vietnam are often not packaged to suit shopping mall environments. Flimsy plastic or cardboard packaging can often damage the value perception of goods. I recommended removing products from packaging to enhance the perceived value or repackaging items into higher quality in order to achieve a higher price at resale and to reinforce your kiosk brand.

Be clear with a strong message about what you sell. Cluttering your stand with products that are outside your 'permitted usage' lease agreement will serve only to weaken your image, confuse your customers and erode centre relationships. The temptation in a kiosk situation is to display as many items as possible to entice shoppers into buying something. Unfortunately, this type of product presentation is more appropriate in a flea market situation or in many eastern countries where bartering for low priced items often takes place.

The problem with overloading your kiosk with too much stock is that it creates clutter and so brings down the **perceived value** of the goods on offer. It makes your stand, products and brand look like they are not worth what you are asking and so your customers expect the price to be lower than the marked price.

The trick is to pitch or position your merchandising standard slightly above the price point of your stock to make it look like the price you want for the merchandise represents good value. If you have volume of stock that is essentially the same, resist the urge to put it all out on display. Instead, take most of it home and refill attractive displays every other morning where necessary.

There is no need to have 12 months worth of stock on your kiosk for daily trading. This 'less is more' approach allows for clean lines and space around merchandise to make it look more attractive and especially enticing to today's consumer.

5. Promotions

Social media is the cheapest and most contemporary way to promote your business. It is the best way to get in touch and keep in touch with your customers and their friends. Content should be informative telling customers about latest stock arrivals or sale events. Collecting Facebook 'Friends' at your kiosk gives you a platform to communicate directly to your customers whenever you want to.

Collecting email addresses for a database can also be a way to prepare you to move into a more permanent retail store down the track and build your brand awareness. A significant customer database can be used for more expensive marketing campaigns or advertising that you may wish to conduct. Make sure your packaging and shopping bags leave a positive last impression and are valued by your customers. Recycled bags with simple stamps or stickers with logos are sufficient.

6. Customer service

Acknowledging customers who walk by or stop to browse at your kiosk with a simple smile and hello is essential to make personal selling connections. Looking customers in the eye is important to engage in a friendly way when greeting them. Outlining the features and benefits of your products to customers is necessary and being able to answer any questions about all products is also vital in the selling process. Closing a sale by asking a customer

'Would you like to take one?' can be enough to finalise your sale in a polite and relaxed manner.

Add-on selling is when the salesperson suggests further products that the customer may be interested in buying due to their related nature to the first sale. For example, let's say you sell a red hat to a customer. Before they pay mention to them that you also have a matching red scarf and gloves that are useful in the cold weather. The customer will either say 'Yes' or 'No' to the suggestion. Often, the customer will respond with 'Yes' and as a result you have managed to double your sales revenue and your profit simply by making a suggestion. This is known as the 'suggestive selling technique' and is used by many retail market leaders.

7. Payment

Offering more than one payment method is essential in today's cashless society. Paying by card is an expectation of today's consumer, especially in a shopping mall environment. If you do not provide this expectation, you may create a reason for the customer not to buy and as a consequence, lose the sale.

In Australia and New Zealand there are low cost options for EFTPOS and credit card transactions such as 'ANZ Fast Pay' or 'Paymate' for payment options on the go. Some of these methods are designed to transact with smart phones and so require no other hardware to incorporate into your kiosk.

Be sure to say goodbye to your customers, collect their details, perhaps by offering an incentive or small gift and invite them to return to your kiosk next time. Treating your customers as you would treat a visiting friend is the best way to understand and conduct your customer service standard.

8. Housekeeping

Your retail stock must be kept in brand new condition and not damaged or soiled in any way. If you have damaged stock, it is best to remove it from your stand and sell it online on websites such as Gumtree (Australia) or Ebay. You will still get more than you paid for the stock and it will not be impacting the *perceived value* of your remaining stock.

Ensure all areas of your kiosk are neat and tidy and your fixtures remain sparkling clean by polishing and dusting daily. *Retail is detail*, so if you focus on these details, the rest will come automatically!

Quick Tips to mall kiosk rebranding

1. **Focus** on who your customers are and creating a positive first impression
2. **Create** your first impression through store design and visual merchandising
3. **Buy** your stock with your customer in mind
4. **Incorporate** perceived value pricing
5. **Leave** a lasting impression with your packaging
6. **Ensure** your fixtures and stock are sparkling clean and soiled stock is removed

Here is a summary diagram of the areas that require focus in mall kiosk rebranding.

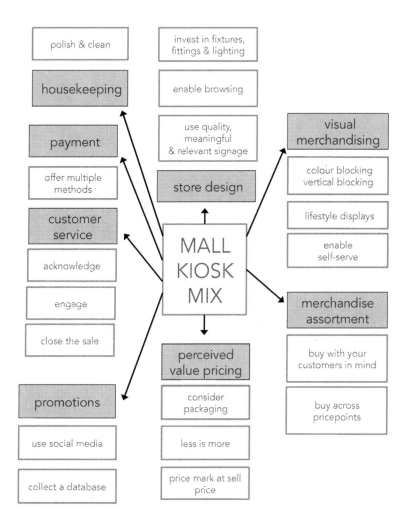

polish & clean

invest in fixtures, fittings & lighting

housekeeping

enable browsing

use quality, meaningful & relevant signage

visual merchandising

payment

colour blocking vertical blocking

offer multiple methods

store design

lifestyle displays

customer service

enable self-serve

acknowledge

MALL KIOSK MIX

engage

merchandise assortment

close the sale

buy with your customers in mind

promotions

perceived value pricing

use social media

consider packaging

buy across pricepoints

collect a database

less is more

price mark at sell price

7-market stall rebranding

Renting a market stall is a truly exciting opportunity to showcase your merchandise in an environment where you are guaranteed foot traffic. If anything, I would say that a marketplace environment is more competitive than any other shopping environment because of the close proximity of stalls and the temporary nature of the selling periods.

The most important starting point for market vendors is to *understand your target audiences.* Know who will buy your goods or services and how that affects your buying and manufacturing (if you are selling direct). However, this can be difficult to plan due to the nomadic and temporary nature of the business. In order to maximise volume of sales you will need to understand the consumer's buying process (CBP) associated with your offer. In other words, ask yourself *who is my customer, how do they shop and what do they want?*

Barriers to buying

Here's an example. In a market environment, apparel stalls often do not have change facilities or mirrors for their customers or perhaps the change rooms are not quite private enough for shoppers to feel comfortable to try items on. This presents a psychological roadblock for consumers, as many are unable to make a decision because they cannot try before they buy.

I call this experience a **barrier to buying.** Anything that creates doubt in the mind of the consumer sufficient enough to turn them off the buying decision becomes a barrier standing in the way of a sale. Great merchants enable the CBP to occur easily and without fuss on every level of the process.

Firstly, really understand the process of buying your products or services from your customer's perspective. Understand how the consumer thinks and feels and what factors influence their decision-making at every point from the first impression to the payment options. Then, design your stall brand and experience to cater for those steps and remove all barriers that may be present.

For example, I attended my own local market recently and approached a cheese vendor. The fellow was friendly, he presented his cheese well and it was quite a nice looking stall. He offered cheese tasting to all that arrived and his cheeses were delicious! However, nobody seemed to be buying. I soon realised why. I hit a massive barrier to buying when I discovered there were no prices on anything. That meant I had to ask the price on every type of cheese I was interested in buying.

I felt bad that I tasted his cheeses with no intention to buy, as I didn't know the price. I couldn't see the vendor's value proposition on his goods without asking and therefore experienced a psychological roadblock. I really didn't want to ask the price, so I had a few tastes and walked away. I wonder how many other consumers did the same thing?

The cheese vendor probably doesn't understand why his tasty cheeses were not selling as in his mind he was offering the best personal service he could to every single customer. Alas, it's because there was a price **barrier to buying** standing firmly in his way.

The market stall mix

Your **market stall mix** is very similar to the *retail mix* outlined in chapter 4. Afterall, you are selling to the same end user but retailing goods and services on a smaller and more temporary scale. Certainly, a more relaxed, creative and perhaps 'boutique' version of the principles outlined in the redesign chapter can be applied.

The location of your stall is of primary importance. Clusters of similar stall types will ensure you get the best foot traffic exposure possible. For example, if you sell coffee, you are best situated near a bakery or at least near other food outlets that complement your offer. Avoid being positioned with gardening products or in the arts and crafts section. This makes perfect sense yet somehow, is not always the case.

The *layout* of your stall should enable the consumer to easily browse, touch, see, feel and even try your products. Providing an experiential dimension to your market stall is important for consumers who many not have been exposed to your brand or your products before. Allow customers to browse without pushy selling approaches, as many consumers do not respond to this technique.

Your stall and *store design* needs to stand out in the crowd and be unique enough to make passersby look and stop. Think about how to make your first impression relevant to your target markets and how to connect with consumers with your overall stand's appearance.

First impressions are extremely important as your customers buy on impulse. If possible, avoid using trestle tables covered in tablecloths or makeshift fixtures. They do not show products in their best light and will detract from your product message. Using low cost recycled handmade fixtures is a better option. Fixtures that are modular in nature and help create interesting and well-built displays that showcase your stock in its best light are appropriate.

Choosing your *merchandise assortment* can be tricky because market stalls often move to several locations on a rotational basis. Buying or making the right products to suit your target markets and the local population (demographic) should be very carefully considered. Market organizers often have all the information on numbers to the market and what demographic breakdown is expected to visit. If not, information on local populations can be found online at the Australian Bureau of Statistics (ABS) website[123] or from the US census bureau at www.census.gov. Being aware of this information will help you buy the right stock in the first place, adding to your success.

Consider that consumers *expect* lower prices when buying direct from a marketplace environment so this impacts your merchandise assortment. It is a good idea to incorporate a diverse approach to your product mix.

For example, you can display a product that gives your stall a point of difference and aids in creating a positive first impression, aligns with your brand and tells consumers who you are and what you do. It may be a highly priced one-off special edition offer, only available at the market. In addition you can incorporate items that have a mid-range price point that screams value to your customers.

To complete your product or merchandise assortment, you might like to incorporate lower priced items that sell in higher volumes to keep you going. Remember that not all products allow you to make the same margin or profit so it is a good idea to spread your margin across different products.

Looking to market leading retailers for guidance on how to incorporate the latest *visual merchandising* strategies is a great way to present your stand. This is called *benchmarking* and gives you an idea of how your standard compares to market leaders who sell similar products to you.

For example, if you sell books on your stall, visit bookstores and see how they arrange their merchandise. Do they organise their books into fiction and non-fiction, alphabetically or by author? If you sell cheese, ask yourself how do cheese merchants arrange their cheeses? All soft cheese together, blues together and hard cheddars together or in similar price points? Do they price all their products? What sort of price tickets do they use? Do they offer tastings?

Go out into as many merchants in your sector as you can and take the best from them to incorporate into your market stall. Today's consumer expects a higher overall standard of retailing and market sellers that incorporate minimum retail standards will sell more.

Exceptional merchandising comes from exceptional infrastructure. Investing in your fixtures will enhance your overall impression.

Using risers that display your products at different heights is essential to incorporate the pyramid shape into your displays.

Arrange merchandise into groups placing larger items at the back and create overlapping pyramids that cascade down to smaller pieces. Colour block your entire stand if your product allows for this style of merchandising and create stories of products that complement each other and cross product categories. This technique is called cross-merchandising and is used by many market leading retailers.

These merchandising strategies create impactful and effective first impressions and allow consumers to shop by colour preferences. Products placed at eye level will gain the most attention from shoppers so where possible, place items that you will make more money from, in those positions.

One of the primary drivers for consumers attending a marketplace is to save money. *Price* is therefore an important factor and it is important that there is a perception of value that goes with your offer. Consumers have an expectation that most products will be cheaper than in a retail environment. This is because the supply chain to market vendors is shorter than in traditional retail supply channels due to local manufacturing and trading and running costs are lower than traditional retailing methods. Today's consumers are aware of these factors and so expect lower pricing.

Another primary consumer driver to markets is exclusivity or scarcity, where products or offers are only available from a particular market vendor. This can add to your brand uniqueness as a market vendor and so should be amplified where possible.

Secondary considerations for consumers attending a marketplace are buying local or organic produce to support sustainable living and experiencing community engagement through social interactions and entertainment that are often highlighted at markets.

These drivers are the reasons that motivate the general public to visit a market and therefore are an expectation they carry with them. Non-delivery of these expectations to the end user through pricing that is too high and uncompetitive undermines value perceptions and inevitably risks consumer disappointment. The result is a browsing consumer who does not buy and perhaps does not return. Be careful not to overprice your goods to avoid disappointment.

Ensure that all goods have ticketed pricing that enables consumers to make purchase decisions on-the-spot and relieve them of the chore of asking the price. It allows you to serve more than one customer at a time and so builds volume of sales. Tickets should be uniform, legible, current and highlight any points of difference the item may have such as '20% cheaper than retail' or 'one only original' or 'environmentally friendly'. These discreet messages can silently help consumers make buying decisions quickly and can sell for you when you are busy with other customers and cuts down transaction times.

Social media is the way to *promote* your market stall brand. Collecting Facebook 'Friends' at the market will let them know where you are and what you offer. It provides a low cost platform to communicate directly to your customers whenever you require.

Collecting email addresses for a database will help prepare for a future move into a mall kiosk or retail store down the track. You will then already have a significant customer database for marketing campaigns and advertising that you may wish to conduct later on. To make your stall experience memorable, you can incorporate value adding through giveaway gifts that are exclusive to your market stall brand.

Make sure your packaging is visibly branded so customers who have purchased goods advertise your market stall brand as they move around. Creating a powerful first impression is the best promotion you can have to attract consumers and tempt them to buy.

Most members of the public are aware that market stall vendors are not retail sales professionals. It is not necessary to have formal retail *customer service* standards. Simple polite manners are sufficient. Acknowledging customers who walk by or stop at your stand with a sincere smile and hello is adequate. Looking customers in the eye is important to engage in a personal and friendly way when greeting your customers.

Avoid the urge to 'hard sell' to browsing consumers. Most consumers do not enjoy this sales approach and generally run the other way, especially when in a relaxed outdoor setting. Outlining the features and benefits of your products is essential and being able to answer any questions that customers may have is also vital. A simple 'Would you like to take one home?' is enough to close the sale in a polite and casual way, which is entirely appropriate in a marketplace environment.

Offering alternate payment methods to cash is essential in today's cashless society. Paying by card is an expectation of today's consumer. If you do not provide this expectation, you will create a barrier to buying for the segment of customers who wish to use their card as a payment method. In Australia and New Zealand, there are many low cost options for EFTPOS and credit card transactions now available such as 'ANZ Fast Pay' or 'Paymate' for payment options on the go.

These methods are designed to transact using smart phones and so, are available at low cost. Be sure to say goodbye to your customers, collect their details, perhaps by offering an incentive, and remind them of the next time you will be at the market place.

These are all minimum standards that today's customers expect and incorporating them into your market stall brand will help you build your customer base and create environments that sell. Who knows, you may be on your way to opening a permanent retail outlet in which case I suggest you turn back to page 1!

Quick Tips to market stall rebranding

1. **Remove** any barriers to buying
2. **Allow** consumers to experience your products
3. **Incorporate** colour blocking into your merchandising
4. **Price** all of your stock
5. **Be friendly** and acknowledge your customers
6. **Enable** multiple payment methods

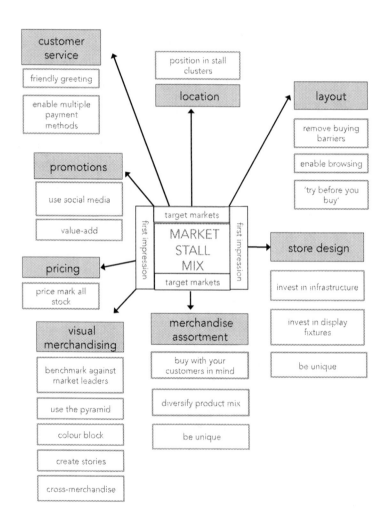

customer
service

friendly greeting

enable multiple
payment
methods

position in stall
clusters

location

layout

remove buying
barriers

enable browsing

'try before you
buy'

promotions

use social media

value-add

target markets

MARKET
STALL
MIX

first impression

first impression

target markets

store design

invest in infrastructure

invest in display
fixtures

be unique

pricing

price mark all
stock

visual
merchandising

benchmark against
market leaders

use the pyramid

colour block

create stories

cross-merchandise

merchandise
assortment

buy with your
customers in mind

diversify product mix

be unique

Acknowledgements

I would like to thank the following people. Dr. Dale Miller at Griffith University for writing the foreword and inspiring and supporting my dream of being an author with such enthusiasm. Dr. Deborah Griffin at Griffith University who accepted me into the Master of Marketing program based on my professional experience. Mark Sutton, General Manager at Paint Place Group of Stores and his amazing team, Bruce, Jen, Jennifer, Margie and Brent for the opportunity and support to implement and measure my best practice visual merchandising program in over 120 stores nationally. The Paint Place group membership who believed in the program, supported and worked so hard to implement the massive changes that have proven so successful across the country. *Thanks for sharing your stories throughout the book.* Amber Hughes from Colonial First State shopping centres and Rebecca Zepackic from Stockland/QIC for the years of work and recommendations to retailers and CML's that have helped me formulate my model. Hundreds of specialty retailers Australia wide (you know who you are!) Graham Randall and Karen from NewsXpress. Steve Whitby formerly of Ducati Australia. Stephanie Tickle from Queensland Museums. Greg McNamara-*You are an innovator and great thinker in the Music Industry.* The Stamford family at Dynamic Music and their customers. Zoom, Sabian and the Godin family. The late Mr. Peter Hayward and his adorable wife Naomi who took me to America for the first time in 2001 and taught me so much in business at an early stage in my professional career. *Ricky* Richard Parsons for showing me how to really sell as a sales rep. Geoff Hyde formerly of Mobex Australia Pty Ltd (Casio) who opened my eyes to brand building and 'the Art of War'. Music retailers Tony Di Caria of Music Express for giving permission to use his mixed revenue example. Sandra Lyndsay, Peter Miller and Matt Gosling for the flow of information about their businesses over the last decade. Mark Meallin, long time friend and mentor in business. Simplot Australia for the training and years earning my stripes as a merchandiser and sales rep. Robbie and Sherree Bennetts, Kate and Rod Watford and Neil Wilks for giving me the opportunity to travel overseas for so many years into retail markets in Asia and the Americas contributing heavily to widening my ideas and experience whilst having piles of fun on tour! *Vegas baby, yeah!* Rotary International. The National Retail Association (NRA) for the decade long partnership in consulting and training delivery. Trevor Evans CEO for his glowing endorsement of the book. Kristine Skippington, Carly Faragher, Maddy Tyson, Missus' Deborah Baker, Karen McCauley, Carlo 'Bello' Disano, Paul Willis, Marlene Barratt, Diana Healy, Haley Bevan and Mike Washington. Joe Hockey MP for the generous testimonial and endorsement of my work with small business. Helen Mary Lewis (H) and Stuart Robert MP for providing me with the opportunity to meet Joe Hockey MP. *Thanks guys, you are stars!* Dr. Steve Flecknoe-Brown, Dr. John Seymour, Dr. Paula Marlton and staff. Natty and family. David, Mellie, *you have always helped me grow.* Emil, Hudda, Alannah and Zoe. Kerrin, Lucy and Bryony. The Stephensons, Eadeh's, Cannons, Metzgers and Grogans for all those beautiful times with good food, wine, conversation and laughter that add so much to my happiness. Trudi (FB) Grogan from Box Advertising for the cover design. Dr. Megan Dalton and Sally Norcroft for your encouragement, wisdom and insight into thinking, writing and studying. You have all added to the book with stories, thoughts and suggestions. Dr. Lorelei Carpenter, Adjunct Senior Lecturer at Griffith University, Gold Coast for the right advice at the right moment and for the final revisions, *Thank you*. Joseph Loiacono for labouring over my references. *Thanks J-Lo x*. Chris Vidal for giving me a retail reader's viewpoint. Last but not least, my family, Pops, Cher, Rhys, Sam, Jill, Jono, Tim, Fi and Dr. Ros Franklin for the unwavering support and teaching me so many things about living, loving and life x.

Baby boomers	People born 1945-1960
Business intelligence goggles (BIG)	The view used to scan your business environment
Brand equity	Amount of notoriety in a brand
Category leader	The business with the most market share in your sector
Carbon footprint	Your business carbon emissions
Consumer buying process. (CBP)	Steps in thinking to reach a purchase decision
Contemporary relevance	Applicable to modern day
Core values	What your brand stands for and believes in
Ecological footprint	The impact you have on the environment
E-commerce	Electronic business/ online
E-tail	Retail online
External brand buy-in	Commitment to the brand from stakeholders outside your business
Fixtures	Slat walls, shelving, gondolas, mannequins, dump bins
Generation Y	The generation born after 1980 (the millenials)
Generation Z	The generation born after generation Y
Global warming	World temperature increases due to carbon emissions
Green retailing	Retailers who focus on environmentally friendly practices
Historic value	The worth in a brand due to its history
Innovation	Revolutionary thinking or inventiveness
Internal brand buy-in	Commitment to the brand from stakeholders inside your business
Internal resistance	Reluctance from people within your business to change

Macro	The bigger picture
M-commerce	Mobile phone purchasing
Micro	The small details
Millenials	The generation born after 1980
Multi-brand retailers	Retailers who offer more than one brand in each category
Multi-category retailers	Retailers who offer products across more than one category. i.e. Walmart
Mystery shop	A secret measurement of your customer service standard by a planted shopper
National brand	A product or retail brand that is recognisable on a national scale
Observational checklist	A list that can be used as a measurement tool
Omni-channel	Revenue coming from several different sources
Positioning	Placement within the Retailscape
Private brand	A generic brand sourced direct from manufacturer
Private label	A generic brand sourced direct from manufacturer
Premium price	A higher price than your competitors charge
Price points	Pricing levels
Primary brand concept	Most important brand ideology
Product brand	The brand placed on products or packaging
Profit Margin	The difference between your buy price and your sell price
Psychic value	Emotional worth
RBM	Retail Business Model
Reassessing	Evaluating again
Rebranding	Reinventing your brand
Redesigning	Constructing again
Repositioning	Altering your place in the surrounding Retailscape
Renaming	Changing your name

Relaunching	Starting again
Retail brand	The store brand
Retailscape	The retail landscape around you
Retained equity	The value left in a brand
Risk mitigation	Minimising risks
R'n'D	Research and development or 'Rip off and duplicate'
Segment leader	The business with the most market share in your sector
Sensory	Of the senses, taste, smell, hear, touch and taste
Servicescape	Your customer service compared to market leaders
SME's	Small to medium enterprises
Stakeholders	All people involved with your business
Strategy	Planned direction and plan of attack
Sustainability	The capacity to endure
Sustainability charter	Enduring plans on paper
Symbolic	Representative of or meaningful
Trend	Shift or swing in direction

Angie Bell is a retail-branding and marketing consultant based in Queensland, Australia. She has over 25 years experience in retail, wholesale, training, motivational speaking and visual merchandising. With qualifications in marketing, business and retail management she is well placed to offer an action plan with a global perspective on best practice to retailers. Angie has helped thousands of businesses reinvent their models earning incredible sales increases in flat market conditions. She has won industry awards for selling skills and academic achievement and her advice has been published in Ragtrader Magazine.[124] Visit her website and blog at theretailreviver.com

'This book is filled with sage advice that will help Australian retail businesses get ahead in an incredibly competitive marketplace. Angie Bell is right, small businesses are the lifeblood of our economy – it is not the size of a business that matters anymore, but the way the business approaches the new economic reality with creative solutions to modern day challenges'.
Joe Hockey-Treasurer, Commonwealth of Australia

'Since 2010, Angie has been the key driver for our Visual Merchandising project for 120 stores with amazing results. Our stores have had increases in category sales up to 60% in some cases due to the layout and in-store direction she has given. I have no hesitation in seeking her advice or recommending her services'.
Mark Sutton- General Manager, Paint Place Group of Stores, Australia

'Inspiring and informative!
A timely aid for the sector and a must read for every retailer'.
Trevor Evans-CEO National Retail
Association (NRA), Australia

Endnotes

1   Miller, Dale, "Retail Branding and Innovation 2012 Course Outline," *Griffith University*, accessed December 12, 2013, https://courseprofile.secure.griffith.edu.au/student_section_loader.php?section=1&profileId=67273.

2   Stevens, Amanda, "Retail Revival: 21 Rescue Remedies for Surviving Turbulent Times," accessed January 8, 2014, http://www.amandastevens.com.au/pdfs/Retail%20Rescue%20Chapters%20 1-3.pdf

3   Sorescu, Alina, Ruud T. Frambach, Jagdip Singh, Arvind Rangaswamy and Cheryl Bridges, "Innovations in Retail Business Models," *Journal of Retailing* 87S (2011), S3-S16.

4   Interbrand, "Best Global Brands 2012," accessed December 12, 2013, http://www.interbrand.com/en/best-global-brands/2012/IKEA.

5   Retail Reviver, "Rebranding Consultation," accessed December 12, 2013, http://www.theretailreviver.com/rebranding-consultation/.

6   Retail Reviver, "Visual Merchandising Consultation," accessed December 12, 2013, http://www.theretailreviver.com/ visual-merchandising-consultation/

7   Liss, Mona, A., "IKEA, in Partnership With American Forests, Announces the Planting of 2 Million Trees Across America," *American Forests,* (April 9, 2012), http://www.americanforests.org/newsroom/ikea-in-partnership-with-american-forests-announces-the-planting-of-2-million-trees-across-america/.

8   ABC Radio National, "A Fairer Food System," (August 16, 2013), http://www.abc.net.au/radionational/programs/bushtelegraph/fair-food/4892372.

9   Hau Lee, "The Triple- A Supply Chain," *Harvard Business Review* 82,10 (2004), 102-113.

10 Weekend Australian Financial Review, *Retail Revolution (*December 27, 2012), 5.

11 Inside Retail, "July Online Spending," (September 3, 2013), http://www.insideretail.com.au/2013/09/03/july-online-spending/.

[12]   Whyte, Sarah, "Postage Costs Soar by 30% as Online Retail Booms," *Sydney Morning Herald*, (April 8, 2013), http://www.smh.com.au/business/postage-costs-soar-by-30-as-online-retail-booms-20130407-2hewv.html.

[13]   Legge, Kate, "Clicks and Mortar," *Weekend Australian Magazine*, (August 25, 2012), 18.

[14]   Pooler, James, *Demographic Targeting: The Essential Role of Population Groups in Retail Marketing* (Aldershot: Ashgate, 2002), book jacket.

[15]   Dee, Jon, "*Small Business: Big Opportunity Sustainable Growth*," Sensis, (2010), 19-23, http://about.sensis.com.au/IgnitionSuite/uploads/docs/Small%20Business,%20Big%20Opportunity%20-%20Sustainable%20Growth.pdf.

[16]   WWF, "Australians World's Seventh Biggest Polluters: Global Report," (May 15, 2012), http://www.wwf.org.au/?4300/Australians-worlds-seventh-biggest-polluters-global-report.

[17]   Randers, Jorgen, *2052: A Global Forecast for the Next Forty Years* (USA, Chelsea Green Publishing, 2012).

[18]   "Warm year as carbon levels keep climbing" *The Courier Mail,* World 25. January 23, 2014.

[19]   National Retail Association, "Sustainability Charter For Retail," accessed December 13, 2013, http://www.nra.net.au/images/sustainability-charter-retail.pdf.

[20]   Retail Industry Leaders Association, "2012 Retail Sustainability Report: Successes Challenges and a Vision for The Future," accessed December 13, 2013, http://www.rila.org/sustainability/sustreport2013/sustainability-report-landing-page/Documents/2012RetailSustainabilityReport.pdf.

[21]   European Retail Round Table, "Sustainable Retailing," accessed December 13, 2013, http://www.errt.org/key-topics/sustainable-retailing.

[22]   Hockey, Joe, *Fadden Forum*. Sheraton Mirage Resort, Gold Coast. July 12. 2013.

[23]   Korda Mentha, "Australian Manufacturing: Redefining Manufacturing," (Publication No. 13-03, August 2013), www.kordamentha.com/docs/publications/13-03_manufacturing.pdf

[24] Google Glass. Accessed December 20, 2013, http://www.google.com/glass/start/what-it-does/.

[25] Elkington, John, "Cannibals With Forks: The Triple Bottom Line of 21st Century Business," *Journal of Business Ethics* 23, no. 2 (2000), 229-231.

[26] Miller, Dale, Bill Merrilees and Holly Belinda Cooper, "Sustainable Corporate Branding: A Typology," in *Contemporary Issues in Brand Research*, ed. George Christodoulides, Cleopatra Veloutsou, Colin Jevons, Leslie de Chernatony and Nicolas Papadopoulos (Greece: Atiner, 2010), 181- 192.

[27] Nedergaard, Nicky and Richard Gyrd-Jones, "Sustainable Brand-Based Innovation: The Role of Corporate Brands in Driving Sustainable Innovation"*Journal of Brand Management* 20 (2013), 762-778.

[28] Sorescu, Alina, Ruud T. Frambach, Jagdip Singh, Arvind Rangaswamy and Cheryl Bridges, "Innovations in Retail Business Models," *Journal of Retailing* 87S (2011), 7.

[29] Ailiwadi, Kusum and Kevin Lane Keller, "Understanding Retail Branding: Conceptual Insights and Research Priorities," *Journal of Retailing* 80, no. 4 (2004), 331-342.

[30] Sorescu, Alina, Ruud T. Frambach, Jagdip Singh, Arvind Rangaswamy and Cheryl Bridges, "Innovations in Retail Business Models," *Journal of Retailing* 87S (2011), 3-16.

[31] Ibid, 3-16.

[32] KordaMentha, "Online retailing: A new era of agile commerce,"(Publication No.12-02, April 2012), http://www.kordamentha.com/docs/publications/publication-12-02-online-retailing.pdf?status=Master.

[33] Muzellec, Laurent, Manus Doogan and Mary Lambkin, "Corporate Rebranding: An Exploratory Review," *Irish Marketing Review* 16, no. 2, (2003), 31-40.

[34] Ibid, 31-40.

[35] Merrilees, Bill and Dale Miller, "The Principles of Corporate Rebranding," *European Journal of Marketing* 42, no. 5/6 (2008), 537-552.

[36] Hatch, Mary Jo and Majken Shultz, "Are the Strategic Stars Aligned for your Corporate Brand?" *Harvard Business Review* 79, no. 2 (2001), 128.

[37] See http://www.nra.net.au.

[38] Art Freedman presentation. *Ace Hardware California*. (Paint Place Conference Hobart, March, 2012).

39   Kapferer, Jean Noel, *Strategic Brand Management: Creating and Sustaining Brand Equity Long Term.* (London: Kogan Page 1997).

40   Merrilees, Bill and Dale Miller, "Principles of Corporate Rebranding," *European Journal of Marketing* 42, 5/6 (2008), 537-552.

41   Muzellec, Laurent, Manus Doogan and Mary Lambkin, "Corporate Rebranding: An Exploratory Review," *Irish Marketing Review* 16, no. 2, (2003), 34.

42   Muzellec, Laurent, Manus Doogan and Mary Lambkin, "Corporate Rebranding: An Exploratory Review," *Irish Marketing Review* 16, no. 2 (2003), 31-40.

43   Shultz, Majken and Mary Joe Hatch, "The Cycles of Corporate Branding," *California Management Review* 46, no. 1, (2003), 6 -26.

44   Davies, Gary, "The Two Ways in Which Retailers Can Be Brands," *Journal of Distribution and Management* 20, no. 2 (1992), 1-24.

45   Aaker, Jennifer, "Dimensions of Brand Personality," *Journal of Marketing Research* 34, no. 3, (1997), 347-356.

46   IKEA, "IKEA Group Yearly Summary FY12," accessed December 20, 2013, http://www.ikea.com/ms/en_AU/pdf/yearly_summary/ys_welcome_inside_2012.pdf.

47   Urde, Mats, "Uncovering the Corporate Brand's Core Values," *Management Decision* 47, no. 4 (2009), 616-638.

48   Pavlina, Steve, "Personal Development for Smart People," accessed December 13, 2013, http://www.stevepavlina.com

49   Starbucks, "Business Ethics and Compliance," accessed December 20, 2013, http://www.starbucks.com/about-us/company-information/business-ethics-and-compliance.

50   Qantas, "Broadening Our Horizons," *QANTAS Annual Review* (2012), accessed December 20, 2013, http://www.qantas.com.au/infodetail/about/investors/2012AnnualReview.pdf.

51   Art Freedman presentation. *Ace Hardware California.* (Paint Place Conference Hobart, March, 2012).

52   Muzellec, Laurent, Manus Doogan and Mary Lambkin, "Corporate Rebranding: An Exploratory Review," *Irish Marketing Review* 16, no. 2 (2003), 31-40.

53   Miller, Dale. *Retail Marketing: A Branding and Innovation Approach.* (Portland, USA: Tilde University Press, 2008), 77-254.

54   Verve Location Powered, "75 Percent of Consumers Use a Mobile Device in the Retail Buying Process: Verve Wireless Study Demonstrates that Consumer Shopping Behavior has Embraced Mobile Devices." *PR Newswire* (December 8, 2011), http://www.vervemobile.com/news/retailstudy/.

55   Kiss Metrics. "Facebook Statistics," accessed December 20, 2013, http://blog.kissmetrics.com/facebook-statistics/

56   Rossiter, John, R., "Brand Positioning: The Three Step Positioning Procedure," in *Perspectives On Brand Management*, Mark. D. Uncles (Prahan, Victoria: Tilde University Press/Palgrave Macmillian, 2011), 61-74.

57   Muzellec, Laurent, Manus Doogan and Mary Lambkin, "Corporate Rebranding: An Exploratory Review," *Irish Marketing Review* 16, no. 2 (2003), 31-40.

58   Ibid, 34.

59   Aaker, David, A. *Managing Brand Equity-Capitalizing on the Value of a Brand Name*, (New York: Free Press, 1992). and Kevin Lane Keller "Conceptualizing, Measuring and Managing Customer-Based Brand Equity," *Journal of Marketing,* 57, no. 1 (1993), 1-22.

60   Major, Jean- Francois, "Successful Small Business Rebranding" (2011).

61   Murphy, John, M., *Branding, A Key Marketing Tool* (MacMillan: London, 1992).

62   Sage, Adam, "What's In A Name? Just Ask the Man Behind the Launching of a Thousand New Identities," *The Times*, (November 9, 2002), 54-55.

63   Pavia, Teresa M. and Janeen. A. Costa, "The Winning Number-Consumer Perceptions of Alpha-Numeric Brand Names,"*Journal of Marketing* 57, no. 3 (1993), 85-98.

64   Kapferer, Jean N. *Strategic Brand Management: Creating and Sustaining Brand Equity Long Term.* (London: Kogan Page,1997), 334.

65   Merrilees, Bill and Dale Miller, "Principles of Corporate Rebranding," *European Journal of Marketing* 42, no. 5/6 (2008), 537-552.

66   Kapferer, Jean N., *Strategic Brand Management: Creating and Sustaining Brand Equity Long Term.* (London: Kogan Page, 1997), 334.

67   Merrilees, Bill and Dale Miller, "Principles of Corporate Rebranding," *European Journal of Marketing* 42, no. 5/6 (2008), 537-552.

68 Shultz, Majken and Mary Joe Hatch, "The Cycles of Corporate Branding," *California Management Review* 46, no. 1 (2003), 6 -26.

69 Keller, Kevin Lane, *Strategic Brand Management: Building, Measuring and Managing Brand Equity* (Prentice-Hall, Upper Saddle River, NJ, 2003), 651.

70 Beaumont, Bob, "Franchising the answer to specialty retail: Bob Beaumont," *Australian Retail,* (May 30, 2013), http://australianretail. com.au/franchising-the-answer-to-specialty-retail-bob-beaumont/.

71 Keller, Kevin Lane, *Strategic Brand Management: Building, Measuring and Managing Brand Equity* (Prentice-Hall, Upper Saddle River, NJ, 2003), 75.

72 Interbrand, "10 Principles of Brand Strength," accessed September 23, 2013, http://www.interbrand.com/en/best-global-brands/best-global-brands-methodology/Brand-Strength.aspx.

73 Miller, Dale, *Retail Marketing: A Branding and Innovation Approach.* (Portland, USA: Tilde University Press, 2008), 77-254.

74 Ibid, 151-153

75 Navizon, "Navizon Analytics: Measure Pedestrian Traffic in Real-Time and Historically," accessed December 20, 2013, http://www.navizon. com/product-navizon-analytics.

76 IKEA, "IKEA Group Yearly Summary FY12," accessed December 20, 2013, http://www.ikea.com/ms/en_AU/pdf/yearly_summary/ ys_welcome_inside_2012.pdf.

77 Stanley, John, *Just About Everything a Retail Manager Needs to Know.* (Perth: Plum Press,1999).

78 Miller, Dale, *Retail Marketing: A Branding and Innovation Approach.* (Portland, USA: Tilde University Press, 2008), 124.

79 Ailiwadi, Kusum, L., and Kevin L. Keller, "Understanding Retail Branding: Conceptual Insights and Research Priorities," *Journal of Retailing* 80, no. 4 (2004), 331-342.

80 Turley, Lou W., and Ronald E. Milliman, "Atmospheric Effects on Shopping Behavior: A Review of the Experimental Evidence," *Journal of Business Research* 49, no. 2 (2000), 193-211.

81 Bellizzi, Joseph A., Ayn E. Crowley and Ronald W. Hasty, 'The Effects of Color in Store Design." *Journal of Retailing* 59, no. 1 (1983), 21-45.

82 See http://www.apra-amcos.com.au.

[83] Turley, Lou W., and Ronald E. Milliman, "Atmospheric Effects on Shopping Behavior: A Review of the Experimental Evidence," *Journal of Business Research* 49, no. 2 (2000), 193-211.

[84] Sankar Sen, Lauren G. Block and Sucharita Chandram, "Window Displays and Consumer Shopping Decisions," *Journal of Retailing and Consumer Services* 9, no. 5 (2002), 277-290.

[85] See www.on.aol.com/video/ces-2012--facecake-swivel-is-a-socially-enabled-virtual-dressing-room-517245023 -

[86] Lam, Alexander, "20 Examples of Experiential Retail," *Trend Hunter,* (August 20, 2013), http://www.trendhunter.com/slideshow/experiential-retail.

[87] See www.birdsnest.com.au

[88] Miller, Dale, *Retail Marketing: A Branding and Innovation Approach.* (Portland, USA : Tilde University Press, 2008), 88.

[89] Ailiwadi, Kusum, L., and Kevin L. Keller. "Understanding Retail Branding: Conceptual Insights and Research Priorities." *Journal of Retailing* 80, 4 (2004), 331-342.

[90] See Insideretailing.com.au 10/7/2013. Red Communications – 'Formats have peaked. Product is the focus'. http://www.insideretail.com.au/2013/07/10/formats-have-peaked-product-is-the-focus/.

[91] Ailiwadi, Kusum, L., and Kevin L. Keller, "Understanding Retail Branding: Conceptual Insights and Research Priorities. "*Journal of Retailing* 80, no. 4 (2004), 331-342.

[92] Ibid, 336.

[93] Kasra Ferdows, Michael A. Lewis and Jose AD Machuca, "Rapid Fire Fulfillment: The 21st Century Supply Chain," *Harvard Business Review* 82, no. 11 (2004), 104-117.

[94] Miller, Dale, *Retail Marketing: A Branding and Innovation Approach.* (Portland, USA: Tilde University Press, 2008), 132-136.

[95] Verve Location Powered, "75 Percent of Consumers Use a Mobile Device in the Retail Buying Process: Verve Wireless Study Demonstrates that Consumer Shopping Behavior has Embraced Mobile Devices." *PR Newswire* (December 8, 2011), http://www.vervemobile.com/news/retailstudy/.

[96] See www.accc.gov.au

97   Hoch, Stephen, J., Xavier Dreze and Mary E. Purk, "EDLP, Hi-Lo, and Margin Arithmetic," *Journal of Marketing* 58, no. 4 (October, 1994), 16-27.

98   Miller, Dale, *Retail Marketing: A Branding and Innovation Approach.* (Portland, USA: Tilde University Press, 2008), 172-181.

99   Chitty, William, Nigel Barker and Terence A. Shimp, *Integrated Marketing Communications.* (Victoria: Cengage Learning), 236.

100   Murray Jr, John, O., and Jan B. Heide, "Managing Promotion Program Participation Within Manufacturer-Retailer Relationships," *Journal of Marketing* 62, no. 1 (January 1998), 58-68.

101   Interbrand Design Forum, "A State of the Industry Report," *Chain Store Age* (August/September, 2009), 15.

102   See www.pemachodronfoundation.org

103   See http://www.tedrubin.com

104   Hoyer, Wayne D. and Deborah J. MacIness, *Consumer Behaviour,* 5th ed (Ohio: South Western Cengage Learning, 2010), 272.

105   Garuda Airlines. "'Familiar Tips" in Flight Digital Menu, accessed 13th Oct 2013.

106   "Looking beyond bread and butter" *Gold Coast Bulletin*, Business 23. December 17, 2013.

107   Chitty, William, Nigel Barker and Terence A. Shimp, *Integrated Marketing Communications.* (Victoria: Cengage), 2.

108   Aaker, David, A., *Managing Brand Equity-Capitalizing on the Value of a Brand Name.* (New York: Free Press, 1992).

109   Chitty, William, Nigel Barker and Terence A. Shimp, *Integrated Marketing Communications.* (Victoria: Cengage Learning), 236.

110   Olsen, Chris, "Brand touchpoints. Brand talk," *Information Outlook,* 7, no. 11. (2003), 38.

111   Davis, Scott, Michael Dunn and David Aaker, *Building the Brand-driven Business-Operationalize your brand to drive profitable growth,* (San Francisco: Jossey-Bass, 2002).

112   Westenburg, Edward, "The Future of Retail Touchpoints*," Cisco IBSG.* (January, 2010), http://www.cisco.com/web/about/ac79/docs/pov/FutureofRetailTouchpoints_FINAL.pdf.

113   Ibid.

114   Uncles, Mark, D. *Perspectives on Brand Management,* 1st edn (Prahran, Victoria: Tilde University Press/Palgrave Macmillian, 2011), 7.

[115] Interbrand Design Forum, "A State of the Industry Report," *Chain Store Age* (August/September, 2009), 15.

[116] Adapted from Art Freedman presentation notes. *Ace Hardware California.* (Paint Place Conference Hobart, March, 2012).

[117] Mc Carthy, Bernice, *4mat Learning System*, accessed December 20, http://www.4mat.eu. .

[118] See http://www.youtube.com/watch?v=6Cf7IL_eZ38

[119] Commonwealth of Australia, "Australia in the Asian Century", *Australian Government White Paper.* (October, 2012), http://www.asiancentury. dpmc.gov.au/white-paper.

[120] See http://www.gbca.org.au

[121] See http://www.foodorbit.com

[122] See http://www.postcarbon.org

[123] See http://www.abs.gov.au.

[124] Smart, Belinda, "Visualising Profitability," *Ragtrader Magazine*, November 4, 2005, 14.